CONOCIMIENTOS
PRESS

SAN JOSÉ TO VIET 'NAM AND BACK

Richard T. García

CONOCIMIENTOS
PRESS

Copyright © 2024 Richard García.
All rights reserved. Copies or reproductions of this book may not be made without permission from the publisher.

Book design by ash good.

Published by Conocimientos Press, LLC
San Antonio, Texas

ISBN: 978-1-961794-01-6

C O N O C I M I E N T O S P R E S S L L C . C O M

To all the loves of my life—
my wife Debora Ana
and
my true-blue friend,
James Prattas.

And to all the young men
with whom I served.

CONTENTS

vii	Introduction
ix	Acknowledgments

San José to Viet 'Nam and Back

3	Who am I?
5	From the barrio
7	Memories y Recuerdos
10	The Trip to 'Nam
12	Long Line of Guerrilleros
15	Pain and Trauma in the Hood
17	Cultural Blinders
19	Music and War Connection
22	Screaming in the Night
24	Yoked to Others
29	Deities and Vision
32	Ever-present Bright Light
34	Honor for My Indian Brother
38	San Jo, We Have a Problem
43	This Was the Only Option
50	The College Years
53	Meeting and Hanging Out With Chicanos
59	Conflicts in Everyday Life
62	Addiction and Trauma—What Is the Connection?
64	The Jungle Fighter
70	Consequences of War
72	A New Beginning
74	Problems in the Homefront
81	Civil Servant
86	Raza Rapture

89	The Spirit in Viet 'Nam
90	Racially Motivated Jurisprudence
92	Cambodian Invasions
99	My Dad is Gone!
100	Spiritual and Moral Injuries
102	Mail Call . . .
114	The Spirit of Quon Loi
117	Music Is Life and Life Is Empty without Music
124	My NVA Prisoner and Ground Squirrels
129	Aquí estoy—Still Surviving
134	Las Guadalupanas of Menudo Hall
139	Truth and Lies of War
143	Real and Fabricated Actions of War
144	Partial Stories and Invisibility of Ethnic Troops
145	The Internal Battle—St. Michael and Me
148	Sources
151	About the Author

INTRODUCTION

When Richard García recognized his future was bleak, he joined the military. For him, employment options were limited to agriculture and labor work with low wages and no advancement. Nearly an adult, Richard had only experienced what it was like to work in those environments, except for that time he washed dishes at a Greek restaurant, before joining the service to honor his family's military legacy.

Garcia pieces his life together, as he reflects on his growing up years, allowing him to enjoy his childhood innocence, returning from the Viet 'Nam War physically, emotionally, and spiritually depleted. Since then, Richard has struggled to understand what he survived.

Now, trapped inside those war memories, he recognizes that his purpose in life is to create a healthy and happy future for his family and himself, and he tries in every which way he can. Yet, he lives and copes with the post-traumatic stress disorder (PTSD) wounds of war. Sometimes he feels disoriented, other times he is triggered to the site of battles that trap and suspends the hurt, and still others make him long for the happy childhood that was his foundation. The trauma of war and its experiences within the destruction and violence he survived often surface at the most unexpected times and in confusing ways.

In this memoir, Richard Garcia's desire is to provide a deeper understanding of those fragmentations. To grasp the ways more deeply in which combat colored his life when he found himself trapped in the jaws of death.

Detachment. Isolation. Repetition.

Like mantras, as his love of music, these concepts reflect old and new coping mechanisms that have placed music at the center of his healing. In the present, he continues re-integrate multi-ethnic music genres into his life, acknowledging that he must contend with the consequences of war for the rest of his life.

—Josie Méndez-Negrete, Editor

ACKNOWLEDGMENTS

Thank you, Creator and Sustainer of all life, for blessing my memories and granting me a grateful heart, peaceful soul, and hands capable of healing through music and touch.

Despite participating in a bloody war, I've learned that I can heal others by laying my hands on them as I have placed them on the drums from age eleven to the present. Most of all, I'm appreciative, happy, and proud to have married my lovely Debbie Ann who gave birth to our two daughters, Elia Maria, and Frida Pilar.

To honor our family, they have been named after members on both sides. Elia Maria was named Elia after my mother-in-law's younger sister, and her first name can be attributed to Elia Robledo Duran and my dad's youngest sister, Maria Garcia Graham. Frida Pilar was named after Frida Kahlo and my maternal grandmother Pilar Perea Diaz. I suggested these names to my wife, Deborah Rodriguez Garcia, because the women after whom they were named are all *chingonas*—strong women.

It is my hope that, like these women, my daughters will also make a difference in their respective communities. They already have begun making their contributions.

Frida Pilar became a pastor who uses her beautiful and soothing voice to celebrate the spirit. She is a gifted artist who teaches art classes via Zoom. As a senior in high school, Frida Pilar tutored a Santa Clara University student in Geometry.

Elia Maria, gifted with a sense of rhythmic concepts like her mother, studied ballet at an early age. As a young adult, she was scouted by the Limón Dance Company of Spain while they were in San José. Also, for a few years she traveled throughout the United

States and Canada with her Bible College dance troupe. Top of her college class, Elia Maria is a Pastor.

Because these strong women came into my life, I am a better man. Without my family, the road to recovery would be more complex and tenuous.

—Richard T. Garcia, May 2024

SAN JOSÉ
TO
VIET 'NAM
AND BACK

Richard in Boyle Heights

WHO AM I?

I am the first-born child of the family. Before I tell my story, let me share a bit about my parents.

Sometime in the 1940s my parents met in the canneries located near downtown San José which included Del Monte, US Packing, and the Barron-Gray Packing Company. When the product shifted from fruits to vegetables, the workers were forced to seek employment at other canneries.

My father worked in the warehouses and mom worked the conveyor belt to sort out defective product. They never worked a production line together, although my dad had his eyes on the woman who would become my mom, when she walked back and forth to carry out her duties in the cannery job.

During layoffs, my mom worked as a waitress at the Borden's Creamery, on the corner of Third and San Fernando Streets, near San José State College. She told me that my dad often stopped by just to say "hello," have an ice cream, and leave.

Before long, he asked her out to one of the movie houses found in downtown San José. That's how the story begins. I was the first-born son.

Mr. and Mrs. Garcia with Richard

FROM THE BARRIO

My parents come from large families. Mom from a *barrio* known as Mexican Hollywood in the Los Angeles Harbor area in San Pedro, California. She was employed in the fish canneries and often spoke about the stench that infused in her skin. To wash it off, she would rush into the house to shower, as if that could remove the odors and stenches from her body. Her brothers were all longshoremen, and among other duties they worked in the harbor loading and unloading vessels and doing ship repairs.

Her brother, my Uncle Fito, a small boy during that time, spent a lot of time swimming in the harbor before that bridge was built. Uncle Fito had his own beach affectionately called BAB or Bare Ass Beach as they didn't have to suit up to swim. The beach has since disappeared and in its place the first suspended bridge in the nation by the named of Vincent Thomas the state assemblyman who spent nineteen years legislating and researching its construction to connect the San Pedro and Terminal Island for freight deliveries.

My dad is from migrant farmworker origins with a family rooted in the Santa Paula area. My paternal grandparents are from Guanajuato. Because of the Mexican Revolution, which was creating and fomenting violence, my ancestors migrated to California in 1910, settling in *La Limoneira*, a lemon grove agricultural camp.

It is not clear to me when my first visit to their lemon grove little house was but as a three-year-old I spent a few weeks at my grandparents' house—Claudio and Andrea. There, I took pleasure in playing with the neighborhood children. My mother's memories differed from my own—she was a city girl, with much to do in the Los Angeles area.

Not long before she died, mom reminded me that she and I lived with my paternal grandparents' family at the Labor Camp. With a tear in her eye, she also said that my crib was a wooden fruit crate with a few blankets in it. Poverty, misery, and hard work was all she recalled.

She didn't stay in that place for too long—she was a city girl. In LA she could get a better job than that of a *campesina* farmworker. Weeding, hoeing, and harvesting was all there was by way of employment.

MEMORIES Y RECUERDOS

My memories simulate old-fashioned movie reels in living color. Among these, the one I will never forget was witnessing my first outdoor pig butchering—something that would often return in battle, as I recalled the butcher climbing on the pig's back and stabbing his throat with a knife. Almost immediately, after slashing the pig's artery, the pig killer carefully directed the blood with a controlled spigot to a large pan.

Nothing went to waste.

We used the blood to make *morcilla*—a blood dish served in tacos with *cilantro* and *cebollas* or what we call *pico de gallo*. Later that day I delighted in eating the most delicious *carnitas*. Aside from such atrocious memories, the *Limoneria* was a dream place, which my paternal uncle Benny called the *"limoznera,"* or beggar. In fact, as kids, my *tía* Rebeca told me that her family lived in *"la miseria."* Stuck in poverty all their farmworker lives.

Still that place has a long history. According to Wikipedia the lemon grove operation was founded in 1893, and quickly become the first large-scale citrus grower in Ventura County. That enterprise began with 431 acres of land and soon grew to 2,731. By 1907 twenty-five employees had been hired. Soon thereafter the place would be touted as the "world's largest lemon ranch."

At *La Limoneira*, the earliest citrus workers were Chinese, Mexican, and a few Anglos. By 1900, much of the labor force was made up of Japanese men. When the U.S. government cutoff Japanese immigration through its "Gentlemen's Agreement," a labor shortage after World War II pushed the growers to search for a new source of labor.

The Garcia Family at the San Francisco Zoo

It wouldn't take long before the growers found their labor pool in Mexican and Mexican American families. They were the ones who would harvest their fields and pick their crops. It was in that very place that my grandpa Claudio Garcia, a Methodist Evangelist, died in an accident. This occurred West of *La Limoneira* on his way home when he was returning from a shopping trip to Oxnard. That unexpected tragedy would not change their lives—they continued to live in poverty. Nonetheless our family found the means and the way to have fun, such as the time we went to the San Francisco Zoo.

In spite of our poverty and its limitations, I am proud of my roots. I am forever thankful for being planted as a seedling in the spiritual soil of East San José where my early childhood was stirred. I'm gratified to have lived in that *barrio*. From that place I carry a repository of community cultural wealth that valued my family and me just as we were.

San José was the place where a higher power than me dispensed my strength to survive. Despite the difficulties I now confront, I take pride in giving my service to the nation, with two tours of duty as an infantry squad leader in 'Nam.

THE TRIP TO 'NAM

Why did I end up there? It might've been family tradition that pushed me in that direction or that options for employment limited me to agricultural work or other types of manual labor. Often, mom talked to me with great pride about her brothers who fought in WWII and Korea. No one talked about war and how it impacted those who served. Glamourized by war movies, their service duty was likened to those films to which we were exposed.

Another influence was the romanticized Hollywood war movies I watched as a kid such as to *Hall and Back* with Audie Murphy and *Bridge on the River Kwai*. So, when I looked at my options, I didn't know enough to explore college. However, the military became the potential source for college money through the GI Bill. Also, in the future I could get a loan to buy a house and secure a government job of some type—the choice was clear. I had learned this from veterans who lived around me.

'Nam would be the way for me. Not only would I find employment in city and state government agencies, but I would also buy property and attend college because of the benefits that accrued in my name for my service.

My Squad in 'Nam

LONG LINE OF GUERRILLEROS

I come from a long line of warriors. In the ancestral sense of my native heritage, as a soldier who fought for his nation, family members who went to war for their country included maternal uncles who fought in WWII: Rafael Diaz, Ramon Diaz, and Ignacio Diaz. Then, there was Uncle Fito—Nature Boy—who was in Korea, and two first cousins who were in 'Nam where I ended.

I thank Nature Boy for showing me I didn't invent myself. With my story, I understand that I am the compilation of all that came before me and will come after—the past, present, and future. I acknowledge that my identity is Mexican native—and that most of us who claim this ancestry are made up of multiple ethnicities—beginning with my maternal grandfather who was born in 1897. My dark brown and very muscular maternal grandfather Ramon Diaz was a Yaqui from Guaymas, Sonora, Mexico. He was raised by a Yaqui family who claimed him as their own. Pilar—his wife—was a fair complected woman from Chihuahua. Grandpa Ramon told my siblings, cousins, and me about his childhood as an orphan during the Revolution.

My maternal uncles, including my Uncle Fito/Nature Boy had dark brown pigmentation and dark black straight hair like Grandpa Ramon. He was a binge drinker, and the entire family witnessed or heard about his violent escapades. I recall that instance sometime during 1967 when my brother Danny who was attending Roosevelt Junior High School in San José, California, heard from one of his classmates that "there's an old wino fighting with the cops at a small park across the street from the fire station on the southeast corner of 18th and Santa Clara Streets." Danny ran

Mr. and Mrs. Garcia with maternal Grandfather, Ramon Diaz

over to see, like a bunch of other kids. And there was our Grampa, throwing blows with San José Police Department officers.

Danny told me he was excited to see the old guy fighting, but at the same time surprised and embarrassed since it was our grandpa who was apparently living at our house like he would do occasionally. When Danny told me this story, and we were already young adults, I too felt embarrassed, but not surprised.

At that point I remembered how my grampa would fight just about anyone that looked at him the wrong way. My pride in our Yaqui heritage became somewhat distorted because Yaquis were portrayed as either fearless Indigenous warriors protecting their Hiakim or exotic Deer dancers, I witnessed that his motivation for combat was in part driven by the effects of alcohol.

Uncle Fito was also a binge drinker. Through his behavior I learned that this type of alcoholism reinforces the multi-generational experience of trauma. In Grandpa Ramon's case, it was from the violent atmosphere he experienced in Sonora, and the many extermination campaigns by the Mexican government to do away with the Yaquis.

But Fito's trauma was Korea.

Grandpa was not a fan of the United States. One time when he was cutting my hair with hand clippers, he very sternly and with much conviction said, "American people don't like Mexicans." Despite those conflicts, by 1940, Grandpa became an American citizen.

He would tell many stories about the difficulties of life in the United States. But his tales were not of war, they were of survival.

PAIN AND TRAUMA IN THE HOOD

Persistent memories tied to intense emotions are connected to my Uncle Fito who would visit us while we were living at 244 Bonita Avenue between the 101 Freeway and the tracks at South 28th and E. San Antonio Streets. Our home was a one room cottage painted a dull white on the exterior, with mustard-colored interior walls and a wooden floor. We slept together in a small bed covered by heavy *quiltas*, or quilts made of cloth remnants by the neighbor who sold them.

In that home, my mom venerated her *Santo Niño de Atocha* statue, and she had a calendar with a picture of *La Virgen de Guadalupe*. Our bathroom was an outhouse next to a huge garden of *nopales* cacti. There were also clotheslines strung between our home and the garden.

At that home, I had much fun playing cowboys and Indians with Dickie, and Bingo Banderas, the landlord's kids. It was in that compound of cottages owned by the kids father—a local preacher who was known for gathering us in his house for Bible study—that we would play barefooted all day in the hot East San José sun. We often re-enacted scenes from cowboy and Indian movies such as Broken Arrow and The Battle at Apache Pass, both featuring Jeff Chandler in the role of Cochise. Mom always said her father looked just like Jeff Chandler, who played the role of Cochise, the name of the county where my Mom was born in Arizona.

"How?" was the word Cowboys used to greet the Indians.

From there a distorted English variety emerge to communicate in both directions. Soon we would tire of the dialogue and run around and throwing pretend arrows and gunshots at each other. Dickie and Bingo Banderas, and probably a couple of other barrio kids reenacted scenes from cowboy and Indians movies. Soon, we got pretty good at sound effects of neighing and galloping horses, gunshots, ricochets, and Indian's screaming at the cowboys during their attacks. We even set up ambushes along the driveway leading to our cottages. We took turns at being the cowboys or Indians in our staged gun battles.

I remember my mom calling us over to a shady tree by our house for Kool Aid and cookies, to comfort our sweaty brown bodies. Sometimes we'd run out to the intersection of highway 101 and San Antonio area whenever a truck hauling fruit or vegetables would overturn, and we'd grab as much stuff as we could, storing them in our tee shirts.

We ran wild and free in our barrio. Nobody had a bike.

The Banderas were perfect for their part because they looked like the Indians we saw on TV—thin, dark brown, but spoke mainly Spanish like I did, although my parents were Spanish English bilingual speakers. Nonetheless, we children mostly relied on Spanish to communicate with the family and in the community.

CULTURAL BLINDERS

In those games we played, my heroes were the White cowboys I had seen in movies at the Mayfair Theater on 23rd and Santa Clara Streets. Sometime later they would be replaced by an *Indio*—Uncle Fito. Those cowboys were left in the dust when my mom's younger brother Adolpho "Fito" Diaz became my hero. When I think of Uncle Fito I am taken back to the Fall of 1951. To those times when my dad carried him into our little house, dressed in his wool uniform, and sat him at our table.

Dad was strong. I loved looking at the pronounced veins in his arms with a tattoo of a cross on his left hand at the base of his thumb and index finger—I often wondered if he belonged to a gang and what its name could've been. It was no surprise to me that he would carry Fito with such ease—dad was powerful! Most inspiring to me was that my parents paid extraordinary attention to our uncle.

As was our practice, when relative or guests visited us, we had a small *barrio* feast which included *frijoles de la olla*, fresh handmade flour tortillas, *nopules* and fried pork chops, but it's not clear to me what we ate. There were times when Uncle Fito spent the night, I imagine we celebrated his visits and presence with our favorite meal.

Later that evening, awaken and in my bed, I caught a glimpse of Uncle Fito's green wool uniform pants, which led me to see that his right pant leg was tucked back to above his right knee with a safety pin. That frightened me. Still with much concern I wondered "Where is his leg?"

The loss of his limb made me uncomfortable. I felt ill at ease to see him hobbling around on one leg in that tiny box of a shack.

Dressed in his Army uniform pants safety-pinned above his right knee and white t-shirt, the next morning Uncle Fito would shave at the kitchen sink, as he sang "Nature Boy" in near perfect pitch. That song, written as a pop ballad in 1941 by George McGraw and recorded in 1948 by Nat King Cole came out the year I was born.

MUSIC AND WAR CONNECTION

As I think back, I can still hear the passion in Fito's voice with every word. That magical intro wrapped inside the memory of my uncle's voice captured the vibe of the song. It displayed the strength of a man who stood on one foot, leaning on the sink, singing as he shaved.

There was a boy,
A very strange, enchanted boy,
They say he wandered very far,
Very far, over land and sea.

With every word, I still picture him standing in front of the sink. That song, launched with its string and flute introduction, and the quality of Nat's voice merging with Fito's linked war and memory for me. *Nature Boy* remains wrapped inside me as my uncle's voice captured a vibe that displayed the strength of a man standing on one foot. From that point forward, Fito became the image of an indestructible soldier. He became the triumphant warrior whose body was medically put together as a result of the perilous events he survived in the Korean War.

Fito's visits were brief.

When the time came for him to leave, my dad picked him up and carried my uncle. He placed him inside our car, then we drove him back to a large hospital where he was housed in an open ward filled with wounded soldiers. Later I would learn that it was Letterman Hospital in the Presidio of San Francisco.

Out of the car, we followed Uncle Fito to this open ward where I saw several men with their legs or arms hanging from metal frames attached to their beds. I said "Hi" to some. A few years later, and after asking over and over, my parents finally told me what had happened to Fito in Korea—he was severely wounded in his right arm and lost his right leg above the knee. I do recall however Grandpa Ramon saying to Fito: "Tell me who cut off your leg," and adding in Spanish "*Yo me los chingo.*" He was ready to throw down for his son.

In later visits, Uncle Fito displayed the prosthetic leg with much pride. He could stand and walk. At his youngest brother's wedding reception, which was held at the Eagles Hall on North Third Street across from Saint James Park in downtown San José.

From watching Uncle Fito, I learned many lessons. Most importantly I took in messages about coping with the wounds and the trauma of war. I didn't understand that his screams, pains, and drinking were linked to war. To the experiences he had survived. There were many visits from which I drew lessons of war.

Grandpa Claudio Garcia

SCREAMING IN THE NIGHT

On and off, Uncle Fito lived with us in the house located at 1688 E. San Fernando Street between 34th and King Road that my dad purchased in 1953. It was much larger than our one-bedroom Bonita Avenue home and it had three bedrooms and instead of an outhouse it had a bathroom. Our new house was white on the exterior.

It was in that houses that I was matriculated in the first grade at Ann Darling Elementary School on 33rd Street and McKee Road. There would be no more outhouse or *nopal* plants for us. Now we had our own inside toilet, even if we had to get in line to use it. Still, in that house and without fail, we often heard the sounds and pains of war.

Their experiences were hard to imagine.

There were nights that my younger brother and I would jump out of bed terrified by the loud screams that could arrive at any time. With much love and concern, Uncle Fito would get up to comfort us and tell us everything was alright. Still, his words didn't sooth our fear or stop us from shaking in our *chonis* underwear.

More often than not, we couldn't get back to sleep.

When all of us were awake later that morning, my brother Danny and I would look down into our breakfast bowl of cornflakes so as not to stare at him. Everyone was quiet at the table, so much so that the crunch of our cereal would later sound like faraway munitions.

Mom and dad were loving toward my uncle, expecting nothing from him. Yet, when Uncle Fito received his VA disability check, he would come over and make us his special Chop Suey. He'd then went to *El Excentrico* magazine's "binding parties," and to some local clubs to continue drinking.

Initially unafraid of his drinking, we saw Uncle Fito with an occasional beer and cigarette which made him appear cool to us, and he was always joking, singing, and teasing my mom. For me, he was the hippest guy. Then, his alcohol binges began to have a negative effect on all of us. We feared he'd get hurt or sick or something, but he pulled through those nasty drunken nights and woke up joking about it as if nothing happened.

One winter night, there were thunderous knocks on our front door. I opened it to see a cab driver holding Fito up. Then, the taxi driver took him inside and spilt him unto the couch, with much care not to hurt him. That's when I began to associate drinking with fear. When I saw Fito on the couch passed out from alcohol, I felt overwhelmed by feelings of helplessness. I was struck by a high degree of inadequacy since I didn't know what to do for him. I was about fourteen and had no experience with how to help a person in such a state. Nobody had taught me what to do. I didn't know how to make black coffee like in the movies for a remedy. I couldn't call my parents since I didn't know where they had gone. His condition made me feel like I was standing next to a dying person. I felt emotionally closed and unable to help him.

That's when I grasped what alcohol could do to a person. Also, that was when I realized that my hero had a drinking problem. In time, I accepted his flaws. I never even imagined I would find myself fighting those war demons.

YOKED TO OTHERS

I am no Frankenstein who was put together by a demented doctor. I didn't invent myself. I'm the result of all that came before me. Little did I know that, after two infantry tours in Viet 'Nam, war would link me to Uncle Fito.

Yet, unlike him, I didn't wake up screaming. I woke up startled in my sleep and had trouble breathing inside thoughts that would place me in a brief but powerful vortex of emotions that I couldn't control. The screams were sounds that come out of a person when pummeled with fists that never end. I could even imagine Fito masking his face with his hands to protect himself from the blows. For it was not the physical punches but the emotional jolts that made me feel like a sack of oranges.

Most of us, who experienced the pain and wounds of Viet 'Nam, buried the trauma deep within. Also, we carry the guilt and shame associated with that war.

In 'Nam, memories of home would give me sanity, particularly that one letter my mom wrote to me in November 1968. At age forty she let me know, she was pregnant. Her letter allowed to imagine that now more than ever my dad's little house on San Fernando Street would be off limits—our home often served as temporary housing for friends and relatives as my parents were known to make space for those who needed housing. Thus, it was our family practice for my brothers and me to give up our rooms. That's how we became accustomed to sleeping on the couch. The benefit was that we could watch television late into the night.

It wasn't only relatives who stayed with us. As best as I can recall, for me that began as early as the third grade. I carry many memories of those who came to live with us—the *arrimados*.

One time a bachelor named Facundo rented one of our rooms for a few months. He rode a bike to work at a nearby tortilla factory known as Best Tortillas. In the evening, using some old English-Spanish manual with pictures, Facundo came to where I slept and asked me to help him improve his English. He was looking for jobs that required the language. In this partnership, he pointed to pictures and asked me how to say that in English, and so it went on until he moved out.

A family member on my paternal side boarded with us occasionally—it was José, my dad's younger brother. He was cool and had great clothes he lent me to attend school dances. Once, while going through his closet, I reached into a sports coat pocket and pulled out a small paper bag. I looked inside, saw some items, consisting of a teaspoon with burn marks on the bottom, some white powder, some matches, and a hankie like the kind cowboys use around their necks. It would not be until much later in Vietnam that I would learn the implications of that paraphernalia. I had no clue where my fingers had been threading.

Around May 1968 while on patrol with my unit—A Company, Second Battalion, Second Infantry Regiment of the First Infantry Division—we were called to an area named The Iron Triangle. That was the first time I had a panic attack. My heart was racing in one of those firefight experiences. It was the first time, we had to call in Air Support to help us get out of a tight situation with the North Viet 'Nam Army (NVA) soldiers who were ten yards away.

The enemy was firing AK 47 machine guns, and Rocket Propelled Grenades or RPG's.

Before advancing on the NVA emplacements with my squad and our M-16's and grenades, the loud and shocking whooshing sound of helicopter gunship rockets flew overhead and were reminiscent of the Fourth of July sounds and explosions. In retrospect, in training we had been instructed that when we found ourselves in bomb blasts, we should open our mouths and yell. The rocket

Base Camp Raid in Cambodia

was near and loud and left me shaking like a leaf in the wind. The explosions were so loud I found myself yelling without control. Not using words but making eerie sounds that made my skin crawl.

Over the two years I spent in combat, actions like this took place many times. I have vivid recollections of the destruction and carry the sound and yells in my memory. The sounds were so profound and deep, they were reminiscent of the tantrums and crying spells I experienced as a child.

In battle and after being discharged, post-traumatic stress disorder (PTSD) episodes readily appeared. The only way I would have respite was when I took myself back to alternative memories I carried.

Among my recollections of war, I have one memory I can never forget. In 1969, while on a night ambush with my unit—the 11th Cavalry Aero Rifle Platoon—a new type of episode appeared just as those ghosts and spirits spoken about in family tales. My partner and me saw what we believed to be two human figures wearing cone shaped hats and black pajamas with AK 47's. As they walked into the ambush kill zone, my heart felt as if I was running a marathon race. I was sweating profusely. My partner and I set off two claymore mines. We fired our M16s. Tossed some fragmentation grenades at the *bultos* or dark figures we saw. Fear created these illusions. Our platoon leader told us "There was nothing there."

PTSD episodes could happen at any moment. The summer of 1970, while sleeping on my parent's couch, I had a bad dream that RPGs were being fired at me from close range (as it happened many times in 'Nam). Those nightmares made real the charge of an RPG hissing loudly, as it sailed along the surface of the jungle and landed as a dud a few feet directly in front of me. But none were as noticeable as those of November 29, 1968, during a two-day battle in a French rubber plantation called *Tierre Rogue* on the Cambodian border. For me, these nightmares produced persistent neck and back pains and headaches for what came to be no apparent reason. Sadly, what began in 1968 through 1970 continues to the present.

When friends and family tell me that the PTSD is noticeable, I isolate.

With several PTSD treatments at the VA, I've become educated on the condition, and later learned that these bouts are experienced differently by Chicano combat veterans. Apparently, there is a difference in how ethnic individuals experience war.

In war, we seldom knew which way was up. Even in the present moment, any sound, or any memory is bound to take me back to various sites of combat. Alum Rock Park became Viet 'Nam's doppelganger for me. It often became the place where I found myself re-enacting war activities as my friends and me climbed to the top of Eagle Rock, running through the woods that took us back into the jungle of our immediate past.

DEITIES AND VISION

I live with memories that continue to surface in my mind. That mid-September day of 1969, when I was assigned to the 11th Cavalry's LRRP-ARP Platoon, as well as that time in February of 1970. I was medevac'd from a patrol near a place close to the Cambodian border called Bu Dop. My body had become listless and achy the day before—but I did not always understand.

The way it began, I felt as if I was suffering from heat exhaustion and would tell the medic of my squad. One time, it was malaria that had me medevac'd to an aid station for medical treatment. On the floor of the helicopter, that medic rode back with me and poured water from his canteen to cool me down. After the aid station confirmed malaria, I was flown to Second Field Force Hospital, on the outskirts of Saigon. My whole body was on fire, but I was still able to walk into the hospital's ward. There, I was treated with quinine and some other medication specifically for round worms.

Malaria is a debilitating disease, and it made me feel like the top of my head would pop off from the high temperature. The next day, I took a shower to cool down. I made my way, holding on to the shower spigot; I felt like the room was spinning with each breath I took.

Throughout this process, I thought I would die.

That would not be the only time, but I soon began to pray for comfort—I prayed the only way I knew how. I spoke softly and directly to God and Our Lady of Guadalupe, pleading them to not let me die in this Godforsaken place. As if in a trance, I heard the high-pitched voices of the old widows from my childhood church,

Resting in Cambodia

Our Lady of Guadalupe in San José, and the choir sang *alabanzas*, praises to God, in a high-pitched Mixtec sounding voices.

Yo creo Dios mío que estas en el altar
Los ángeles cantan y alaban a Dios
Bendito, bendito, bendito sea Dios
Los ángeles cantan y alaban a Dios

Dressed all in black, the singers were dispersed throughout that small church, where a few barrio dogs gathered to drink from a puddle below the leaky faucet at its entrance. With that recollection came a vision of a procession of men carrying the figure of the *Virgen de Guadalupe,* followed by the *Santo Niño de Atocha*—I saw these visions everywhere, with their specific lights and reflections.

EVER-PRESENT BRIGHT LIGHT

Deep in that illness, I was in and out of consciousness. During that malaria shower, I saw a bright light emanating from a window at the upper corner of the shower stall—it looked brighter than the sunlight and it kept pushing through. A short time later I woke up in bed. Someone told me I had collapsed and was carried out by a male nurse.

Two days later I walked out of the ward and caught a ride on a Caribou cargo plane back to Quon Loi. While walking down a corridor of the old French Colonial two-story building, I saw what appeared to be a Latina doctor with a Spanish surname in green fatigues. She walked toward me with a pair of medic's scissors and pen in her breast pocket. Her presence calmed me, and I nodded saying "Hello, mam" when I passed, I detected she was a captain. In any case, with a smile of encouragement, she made me feel whole from that moment and I wondered if I had seen God or the *Virgen de Guadalupe*.

I wondered about this and sought answers in relevant passages of the Bible—the way some say you can see Him, and some say you cannot. Several came to mind:

Genesis 32:30: And Jacob called the name of the place Peniel: "For I have seen God face to face, and my life is preserved."

Exodus 33:11: "Thus, the Lord used to speak to Moses face-to-face, as a man speaks to his friend."

God and Moses at Exodus 33:20: Said, "you cannot see my face, for man shall not see me and live."

While contradictory to each other, these passages—33:11 and 33:20—deem that you cannot see God unless you die. Still, the vision of that sacred image in the sun and the Latina figure provided grace in my sight, and "showed me Your glory," as the Lord said, "I will make all 'My goodness pass before you, and I will proclaim the name of the LORD before you. I will be gracious to whom I will be gracious, and I will have compassion on whom I will have compassion.'"

Clearly, I thought, "to see him would be to leave this world and only see Him when I die."

I resolved that I may have seen His goodness pass before me, in the bright lights and a smiling face of a brown woman which was followed by spiritual and physical healing. But I never found a scripture that said you cannot see *La Virgen* manifest in the form of that Latina Army captain that I saw on the way out to the hospital. Unlike *La Virgen* did with Juan Diego, Our Lady didn't speak words of comfort such as "am I not your mother?"

Her smile and nod gave me the strength to go on. I still carry those memories and recollections of war. At any moment I can find myself in battle.

HONOR FOR MY INDIAN BROTHER

Forever in my mind. October 27, 2014, the memory I carry of Ervin Harris came to me in Columbus, Ohio.

I'd met Harris during my first tour in Vietnam sometime August 1968 when he was assigned to the infantry rifle squad, I was leading in Vietnam with the 1st Infantry Division. He was drafted a year before by the Army on his 20th birthday. An Ohio boy, he was athletic, muscular, and bright. We served in that war for several months. He valiantly fought the enemy.

Sadly, in that French rubber plantation along the Cambodian border, on November 29, 1968, Harris, along with about twenty-five U.S. soldiers, was fatally wounded when hit by RPG fragments to the head—he was about ten yards from my position.

Two weeks before he was killed, Specialist 4th Class Ervin Ellis Harris had turned twenty-one years old on November 13th. Harris had been in my squad one month and was assigned company commander radio operator for two months and one week when we lost him in Binh Long, South Vietnam.

After my second tour, while with the 11th CAV in 'Nam, I returned to California where I would live after being discharged, where I would study, work, and raise a family. I would move with my family in 2006, and, when I became employed as a Civil Rights Investigator my family and I moved to Ohio.

Ervin remained in my life. Forever present in my thoughts.

At my new home, one brisk fall Ohio morning, I received a call on my office phone from an Ohio assistant attorney general. He asked if I knew Ervin Harris. I answered, "Yes. I was with him when

Richard and Deborah Ann Rodriguez Garcia

he was killed." The person who called me turned out to be Ervin's childhood neighbor in Oregon, Ohio, near Toledo, close to Lake Erie, where they had spent much time together as children. Ervin was about five years older than his friend. That call came with an invitation to attend a memorial service he had organized for Ervin and five other men who had died in 'Nam—all had attended Clay Senior High School. We were 1966 high school graduates—Ervin from Clay and me from San José High School in California.

To celebrate his life, my wife Deborah and I drove to the Oregon VFW Hall where a dinner and memorial program were hosted by the organizers. There, I reunited with my former platoon commander. One of the guys who had been in my squad that fateful November day was invited. I had not seen them since the day they sustained gunshot wounds. That's when they were medically evacuated for those severe battle wounds.

The next evening, my wife and I met Ervin's Native American family. We had dinner with them.

They had many questions about Ervin's death.

My assignment, I believe, was to tell them the truth.

The Harris family told me about the time soldiers came to their door to advise them of Ervin's death in combat, late November 1968. After that, they toured me through their humble home where thirteen kids were raised. Harris's oldest sister told me the kids had worked on the family commercial fishing boat on Lake Erie. I thought "that must've been the reason Ervin developed a muscular body from pulling in fishing nets."

Harris's family embraced us as part of their Native American family. The next day, we went to Ervin's gravesite where Debbie Ann insisted, I lead a l prayer for the family. Did not anticipate this request, but when it came, I became stiff and gasped for air. Made every effort to get words out. They finally came, and I prayed for him and all of us who continue to wage war at home and in our respective communities.

Ervin's plaque read "November 29, 1968"—the date of his death. The roller coaster of war lives inside me in my everyday life.

Ervin E. Harris and Viet 'Nam War Memorial

SAN JO, WE HAVE A PROBLEM

July 1970. When I returned home, I felt like an outsider. With two tours in 'Nam as an infantryman, things had slowly changed but even to this day I act differently, because I haven't always had the awareness to understand the ways war changed my inner core or my ability to critically reflect and understand war's impact on me and my daily life.

I flew to California from the Cambodian jungle in a different type of aircraft, freeing me from military life. With no firm plans, other than to attend college and get a job, I was one of many in this situation. Back in civilian life, I would come to learn that I carried more baggage than the one I physically had. Much of it was embedded in my mind and soul.

The day I arrived home, it was an extremely hot day. I rode the Greyhound from Oakland to San José. I carried my duffle bag containing all my belongings. From the bus station, I caught the First and Santa Clara Street bus, which was filled with people riding to work, going to school, or keeping appointments, but for me it was a ride home. When we reached the corner of 35th and Santa Clara, two blocks away from my dad's house, I got off the bus.

Man. It was a joy to see the area; it was just like I left it.

A young, nice looking Mexican woman asked me if I wanted a ride.

"No, thanks," I said, "I'm a block or two away from home."

That was my welcome home parade.

Elated to have returned, I was so happy to see my loving parents and siblings. I don't think I've ever been on such an emotional high.

Ever. Not ever.

Dad let me live with them—my five siblings, and mom. The house was small, and I slept on the couch. They were as glad to see me alive as I was to see them. Also, it took a while to adjust to eating the *real* Mexican food made by mom. A month or two went by and I was still on the couch.

One early morning, I woke up wheezing heavily. I got up, opened the door for fresh air, and in a few minutes the wheezing stopped.

I did not realize that my breathing problems were associated with that never-ending dream—displaying a crystal-clear representation of the battle of November 29, 1968, where I found myself in that rubber tree plantation in Loc Ninh. I could see an NVA soldier clearly firing an RPG at me from about fifty yards away. The past melded with the present—there was a projectile floating about 3 to 4 inches above the floor of the plantation, coming toward me. As the rocket floated my way, I saw the debris on the ground separating, landing about ten feet in front of me before it stopped. A few seconds later, me and my buddy Ed Gann vaporized that soldier with our weapons, and then assaulted his emplacement, and cleared it with grenades. I could see bits of clothing and flesh shoot out of the bunker portal—it was as if I was there again. Those dreams held me hostage inside 'Nam years.

However, at home in East San José, I got up and went about the business of working on my light blue 1968 Volkswagen. This was the vehicle in which I drove around aimlessly during those days, and into the night just to have something to do. To mellow out I smoked a lot of pot to get by. Then I enrolled at a community college, to get some type of income from the GI Bill, which turned out to be a mere $175.00 a month. For that I had to carry twelve semester units. It wasn't much money for a young guy with personal needs, but I kept up with classes. I did the best I could.

In class, I drifted in and out of war scenes. Participated only when I was irritated or annoyed by a self-righteous Chicano.

At home or in school, I lived inside the nightmares of Viet 'Nam. Still that prevalent dream slightly subsided in the last few years, but the nightmares continue to manifest in other ways: Sometimes I smell the clothing of NVA that I had dragged out of streams, or bunkers. Other times I see the corpses and have death recollections of those I killed with my knife, after they had been wounded in my ambush patrol in Cambodia while with the 11th Cavalry Aero Rifle Platoon.

In 'Nam and at home, I dealt with those problems as best I could, but self-isolation was the best medicine. Time was on my side. Things would improve.

So, when I was twenty-one, I met a great Baptist girl when I was living in an apartment, in the San José State area, with two friends who were Viet 'Nam veterans. We would often have friends over and listened to popular rock and Latin music albums.

One time, a friend brought his sister Debbie with him who was about eighteen, and he also brought his cousin. All of them were singers, musicians, and actors in the local Chicano scene. I was always excited to talk about music with them and at times practice since I now had my first conga and bongos. They asked me if I'd like to perform with their newly formed group, I excitedly agreed, and began rehearsals. I always felt great whenever I'd saw her and was happy that we became friends and bandmates. Soon, Deborah Ann would become my emotional anchor. Debbie and I got married when I was thirty-two. I thank God for her every day. Without her I'd be dead or lost.

Nonetheless, the war-time nightmares continue and there are times I wake up startled with my body burning up, not perspiring just hot. Sometime later, the wheezing changed to spasms in my throat that left me nearly out of breath and made me feel like I was choking.

Previously diagnosed with asthma by my healthcare provider and the Veterans' Administration Hospital (VA), they would later establish I had Vocal Cord Dysfunction (VCD); that's what gave me the feeling of being choked. This condition has compromised my safety, especially while driving as I have to get out of the traffic and pull over—get out of the car and wait for the event to pass. The sensation I felt was a combination of being choked, and being taken down underwater by a large wave, until I caught my breath. This can happen anywhere, even at work, and it's become quite embarrassing. I've dealt with the situation as best as I could, but I've learned to wait it out until my body and emotions calm down.

Through therapy at the VA, I've learned to identify episodes which begin with chest pressure before the choking arrives. Filled with nervousness, most times I'd go to the nearest bathroom, take off my shirt and tie, and sit in a corner of a stall, until the stridor event passes.

Over a forty-year period I've taken up my health concerns up with the VA, and they say I am over-exaggerating those exhausting post-traumatic stress disorder (PTSD) symptoms. In fact, the first time I got any indication I had vocal cord issues was when I sought help at a local emergency room, and the treating doctor said, "You don't have asthma. You suffer from classic PVCD symptoms," then he gave me a small bottle of Xanax, instructing me to take one after the next event, but not before directing me to "Get to an ENT specialist."

That's what I did. That was exactly the diagnosis given by a Speech Therapist.

Since 1970, I have sought treatment and disability compensation for this condition, since it is associated with the violence I experienced in 'Nam.

Presently, I am preparing for an appeal, and retaining legal counsel to contest the VA's last denial of a compensation rating increase. And the battle at home continues, as folks wonder but fail to ask what it was that I experienced.

On the other hand, and most clearly, I have been asked how I see PTSD by my assigned care providers. I respond that "it's like having an attack dog over which I have limited control." Medication helps as well as raising my right hand up to the Lord and asking for His help, until the dreams and throttling stops. The trauma of PTSD is unpredictable and unending. A close friend and former buddy from the Army who is a specialist in PTSD often reminds me, "That shit never goes away." Now, in my own body, I know what my friend meant. Time served gave me more than I bargained for.

THIS WAS THE ONLY OPTION

Why war? There was no other choice for me. Most of the time my high school grades were bad. I would often skip classes to cruise with friends who had cars. Still, I graduated May of 1966.

That summer, I passed the months taking the bus and walking around job searching, with virtually no plans. Downtown San José in mid-June 1966, I asked several small businesses if they had any work. I got hired as a dishwasher at Maris Greek restaurant— two doors down from the UA Theater on First Street. The owners— the cook and his wife who spoke with heavy accents—were kind and provided me free meals at the end of my shift.

During one of these meals, I learned the restaurant owners were Greek immigrants. The cook offered to train me. That wasn't what I wanted to do the rest of my life. So, I found myself telling them stories about former high school classmates and the types of good paying jobs they had.

With not much of a future ahead of me, I went to the Army Recruiter located at the San José Greyhound Bus station. Several of my classmates had been drafted or joined the military. I recognized dish washing held little promise. After exploring my options, I soon enlisted. Then, I returned to work, and gave notice to my employers that I would be leaving for the Army early July.

The owner's wife sternly commented, "Are you happy?"

I didn't know what to answer. But, when I was hired at Maris Restaurant, I recalled that being a dishwasher wasn't a career choice. It was more of a survival option for me. I needed money to buy a car and clothes, while living at home.

The owner/chef and his wife/manager worked very closely as a team. She organized the place, and he was the chef. They were always neatly dressed in their whites and the place was spotless, even the front window which faced South First, the busiest street in downtown San José. My job was to keep the pots, pans, plates, and utensils clean and sanitary for serving the guests. By the time I joined the Army, the chef had offered to train me as a cook. When he asked me, I looked back at him with a less than enthusiastic stare since I really had not developed an obligation to remain as part of their team. I was not interested in restaurant work. Convinced that the military was my only option, I enlisted even though I felt I had betrayed this old hard working traditional Greek couple. It was like quitting the basketball team in high school.

Still, I decided to move on without providing an answer to them. Others who asked, I would give no firm response.

On July 10, 1967, I took the Greyhound to the Oakland Induction Center. Surprisingly, there were police confronting several protesters at the building's entrance. Much later, I got a physical examination and was given a meal ticket for lunch at a nearby restaurant.

After the swearing ceremony, I was sent to basic Army training at Ft. Bliss, Texas. That was the first ever plane ride I took—Oakland to the El Paso where Ft. Bliss is located. The barracks were my home for about three months—July to September—and I tanned nicely while there. The soldiers with whom I was training were mainly from the Southwest: About two dozen Mexicans, a few Navajos, fewer Blacks, and many White guys.

Toward the end of training, I was given a liberty pass to go into El Paso for the day and I set off with two guys from California. For a while, we walked the plaza at the center of town in our starched khakis, checked out a couple of beer joints, and went to a restaurant for some decent Mexican food.

After basic training, 90 percent of the guys received infantry training orders to Ft. Polk, Louisiana, also-known as Ft. Puke,

Richard Leaves San José—Family Send Off

Lousy-ana. Their fate was sealed. I felt relief since I was assigned to training at a radio school in New Jersey and not Infantry training. The drill instructor wasn't directing the Viet 'Nam probability toward me. He was matter of fact about it, he said in a rather sadistic tone. "Most of you guys are going to die over there." The guys who were assigned to Ft. Polk, were deeply saddened about their prospects. I felt sad for them. I was sent to Ft. Knox Kentucky for tank training. That made it highly certain that my assignment would be to Viet 'Nam. I was consumed by sadness when he uttered,

"For sure, the next stop would be Viet 'Nam." That was what the drill instructors told the group.

As fate would have it, I was sent to Ft. Monmouth, New Jersey—but it was only for a short training stint. I thought I had lucked with the gig as a result of the radio communication training, then I was sent to Ft. Knox, Kentucky for Armor School tank training. That wouldn't be the end of my journey, there would be more movement for me.

Again, we left the driving to them, and I made my way to the Greyhound ticket counter. I took the bus from Ft. Monmouth, New Jersey to the New York City Port Authority.

Sheltered in my San José experience, I was highly surprised at the presence of effeminate looking young males at the station. Another thing I will always remember is hearing Linda Ronstadt's "Different Drum." 'What a fine voice,' I thought as the Greyhound bus pulled into Ft. Knox.

We arrived in the early morning in the middle of a blizzard. Something I had never experience or seen in my life. The frigid climate of the area into which we arrived truly surprised me.

In training, I drove tanks and qualified for all their weapons, so Armor Training was exciting.

With only one Chicano from Texas, by the last name of Castro, my fellow soldiers were mainly Black and White. I slept next to a very friendly Black guy from Georgia. He and I spent time at the PX shopping for stuff, playing Motown music on the jukebox, and spit shining our boots in the barracks. There, he asked me,

"So, what good Mexican singers are there?"

I answered "Trini Lopez."

He responded with a roaring booming laugh. "Ha, ha, ha ... Trini Lopez? Shiiiiit!"

During our last week of tank training, we had an assembly at Patton Hall. The speakers were officers and men who had served with the US 11th Cavalry in 'Nam. We learned that they had nothing promising for us young inexperienced Armored Cavalry soldiers.

Next, my orders were to show up at the Oakland Army Terminal for Viet 'Nam. I was scheduled to depart March 3, 1968. However, before that I went home on a thirty day leave just as the snow began to melt in Kentucky. I spent my leave time with my parents and siblings.

In the Bay Area, with buddies I met at Ft. Knox, we went straight to Haight-Ashbury, where I scored a ten-dollar lid. We had a good old time, despite being called baby killers by some long-haired goons. To avoid trouble, we decided not to fight them, so we kept partying.

When I left San José, it was a typically crisp and cool but sunny winter morning. I never thought that I would cry in front of the family, including Uncle Fito who came to see me off, but I couldn't hide my feelings. Surprisingly, my mom placed an unforgettable salty warm kiss on my lips—an unusual show of affection for a Mexican mother.

From a friend's car window, I waved goodbye. For me, the war was just beginning.

At Travis, we caught the plane to 'Nam. In the pocket of my pants, I still had what was left of the weed. When we were told that the Military Police (MP's) would be coming on board to search the plane with dogs. I got up went to put the stash in the magazine pocket of another seat in front of mine. I went to the bathroom and made sure those dog handlers came through and found nothing. All the way to our first stop, Alaska, we smoked weed in the bathroom.

Finally, we arrived at the Bien Hoa Airbase. We were bussed to a camp where we were assigned to our units and some of us were sent to a mechanized infantry company.

"Damn, I thought I was armor, not infantry. Why send me there?"

It turned out that only one guy in our group was assigned to a tank company. I would spend the next year in the field on large operations, where we conducted Search and Destroy missions, nighttime ambushes, and road security.

On that tour of duty—1968-69—I never got shot. However, many of the guys around me did and many died.

Richard Leading the Troops

THE COLLEGE YEARS

Re-introduced to the changing culture of the *barrio*, my return was surreal. At home, I navigated civilian life in San José, and enrolled in the Mexican American Studies (MAS) program at San Jose City College, where I would re-acquaint myself with old friends and make new ones.

One impressionable moment I recall was watching "I am Joaquin." A movie based on a poem by Chicano activist Corky Gonzales that celebrates Chicano identity. To my surprise, the music credits listed Felipe Rodriguez whose guitar skills had always impressed me. I later learned that he was an actor with *Teatro Campesino,* but he never told me about the movie.

After attending a local meeting at the *Huelga Center* on North First Street in San José, I went to the Lucky Grocery Store on Story and King Roads to join the picketers in their call to boycott non-union grapes. The first guy I ran into was my dad's younger brother, Jose Garcia; I had not seen him since my return home. In the parking lot, we leafleted shoppers coming and going to their cars. Most embraced our presence.

Not too much later, I heard that a Chicano Moratorium was slated for August 29, 1970, in East LA. I decided to go. What was there to lose? If I had traveled over 7,800 miles from Saigon to Oakland, I could attend an anti-war event in Los Angeles. In my VW, my friend and I drove to LA and soon found the location—it was right off of Whittier Boulevard.

When the march concluded, I sat on a grassy field listening to speakers and Chicano Movement music. My friend Ben was performing with one of the groups. A young Chicano I met in San José asked me to go with him to buy some beer at the corner liquor store. So, we walked on over.

Then, out of nowhere, some guys ran out of the store with stolen wine bottles. Someone broke the front window from the outside.

"Leave the beer. Let's get back to the park," I told my buddy.

A few minutes later, a large contingent of the LA Deputy Sherriff's riot control unit began to clear out the park with their batons and tear gas, busting the heads of anyone who wasn't clearing out. When I got a whiff of "tear gas" I got a major 'Nam flashback. Immersed in fear, my buddy and I ran to where we had parked the car and drove to my aunt's home in Wilmington.

Beside the 'Nam induced PTSD, my college education was disrupted by an unsettling and fragmentary self-defeating relationship with a woman I knew in high school and with whom I attended the community college. Due to many conflicts, this ill-conceived romantic relationship failed, left me emotionally shattered. Of course, I took the blame for all the mess. To calm myself and to self-medicate, I found comfort in pot smoking and those VW long solo drives I took.

Despite an emotional and confused state of mind, as it turned out my community college grades were good enough to transfer to San José State, January 1971. Influenced by Carlos Castañeda paperbacks, my major at that time was Anthropology. To complete my work and do the assignments, I spent long hours at the library, but most often I was unsuccessful because of those intrusive and unpredictable flashbacks. Insecurity and my Milpitas Ford Plant's swing shift job, to which I rode my ten-speed bike, negatively impacted my academic performance.

PTSD was wreaking havoc on me. Sometimes I remained awake three-to-four days at a time, just like in 'Nam. Not long after that, I dropped out of San José State and the terrible grades I received cast doubt on my ever getting a degree. By 1986, I had gathered enough credits to get an Associate of Arts. At the graduation ceremonies at San Jose City College, we were interrupted by Vietnamese graduates protesting the appearance of Tom Hayden, an anti-war activist, and a member of the Chicago Seven. Despite the disruption, to celebrate we had a pizza party at House of Pizza close to the Civic Auditorium—my daughters were babies at the time.

My formal education stopped. I focused on work.

It wasn't until I became a vocational instructor in Gilroy's Center for Employment Training (CET) teaching Landscaping that I contemplated the continuation of my education. CET had hired me because of my years of experience working for the City of San José as a landscape laborer in the early 1970's. At CET I gained a noble occupation, teaching marketable skills in English and Spanish to farmworkers and displaced service and industrial workers.

While employed at CET, I participated in a program designed for bilingual vocational educators at the University of San Francisco (USF). If you had a BA, your participation would award you an MA. Given this incentive, I enrolled to complete a Bachelor of Arts at Capital University, Columbus, Ohio, graduating May 2013. After this, I petitioned USF for the master's degree. To give me the MA, the institution had to reconcile the records of another Richard Garcia from Florida.

When the issue was resolved, I walked with the graduating class of December 2013. The education bug had inspired me to continue my preparation, and to further my education I searched programs of study. At Ohio Christian University, I matriculated for a master's in business administration (MBA) program. After a grueling two years, I received my degree on May 5, 2014.

So, there you have it, as fragmentary as it may appear, I finally completed a higher education. The first-born child of a working family, of farmworker background from East San José, did all he could to complete four degrees—AA, BA, MA, and MBA. I did not seek further higher education. Life would become my education.

Still, I took on a new educational path and focused on music. In the beginning, this would be from records, and then with a few Bay Area Latino percussionists, and some Cuban and Puerto Rican Masters. I played with a few Latin Rock bands in San José and continue studying Latin rhythms.

MEETING AND HANGING OUT WITH CHICANOS

Music became my relief from the damages of war. I played with some well-known groups in San José and the Bay Area.

First of all, while settling into college life, I became the first percussionist for a San José group named *Flor del Pueblo*. My initiation started by jamming with a few of the members and my friend Ben, who was the bass player. That bass had a history. It was one of the instruments checked out by Ben from Roosevelt for the summer music classes. That was when Roosevelt Jr. High was torn down, but he was able to keep the instrument.

During one of our musical sessions, I met my friend Felipe's younger sister, Debbie Ann Rodriguez, a gifted musician, and vocalist. I was taken by her beauty, calm spirit, and excellent voice. I remember telling one of the guys, "Debbie is really cute," to which he responded. "You and my cousin? Never!"

With our *Raza* community contacts, we started doing gigs as *Flor del Pueblo* all over the Bay Area. We soon recorded a 45 at Tiki Record Studio on 18th and Julian Streets. The original vinyl is still in my possession.

Soon enough the group expanded in its number of players which included members of another San José musical family. I played with them for some time and began to feel like I was less valuable to the group—it could have been my nonalignment with their political rhetoric. I would discover that although Ben and I were in on the group's album recording session, our parts were excluded from the credits. Prior to that recording, I told Ben how

Deborah Rodriguez with Flor del Pueblo

Flor Del Pueblo — Early Days

First 45

Rudy Madrid, Ben Cadena, and Richard Garcia

I felt about aligning myself with the group's communist rhetoric, since I had just spent two years chasing communist who were trying to kill me.

It wasn't long after that I was kicked out of the group. I think it was by the members who were part of the earlier expansion. Still, I remained friends with the Rodriguez family, and occasionally practiced with them. Soon after getting kicked out of the group, *Flor del Pueblo* broke up. However, some of the original members kept playing together. Unphased, I played with local bands among them Rudy Madrid and the Vern Brooks Big Band—also known as Bernie Fuentes.

Debbie Ann and I were married. I couldn't have been happier.

Sometime later, because the music soothed my soul and inspired by spirit, my repertoire expanded to include Gospel Music. This happened at a Midwest Pentecostal mega church in Ohio, where my daughters were studying in a Bible college. As an undergrad at that time, I was also at Capital University in their Music Conservatory's World Music Ensemble. These two musical disciplines allowed me to deepen my knowledge and learn additional techniques on Latin Percussive instruments. From 2006 through 2017, I performed with world-renown Latin and Gospel artists. I would eventually get recruited by local Puerto Rican and Venezuelan bands to perform and record with them. Also, I became involved in the planting of a Spanish speaking ministry's worship band.

These experiences were both a taxing and rewarding period of study and performance. They were challenging because I had to develop my sight-reading skills for Latin charts, and I learned how to play in a black Gospel Pentecostal worship band.

CONFLICTS IN EVERYDAY LIFE

In 1977, some years after returning from 'Nam, I was recruited as an officer by the San José Police Department. The community had entered into a consent decree as a result of a discrimination lawsuit when they pushed to hire Chicano cops. I met their criteria for the job—tall enough, with light complexion, and hazel eyes.

After completing basic police academy, I was assigned on patrol with a field training officer. In the beginning, everything was promising. I took on police culture as something special.

All that drastically changed as PTSD began to manifest on the job. The first time it happened was when my trainer and I responded to a call that came in at 1:00 in the morning about a man brandishing a knife. As we pulled up to the complainant's address and approached the house from which the call came, we found a young Mexican man pointing a hunting knife in a threatening manner. He lunged at my partner. This guy looked like he was "blasted," or intoxicated on PCP. Since I didn't have a radio on my belt, I went to our patrol car and called for assistance to deal with the crazed man.

With our batons, we finally subdued and handcuffed him. After having detained him, I came to the realization that I could've easily shot and killed him.

Once I got home, I tried to sleep, but my mind raced, and I had trouble breathing which resulted in a few sleepless nights. It was after that incident that I began to doubt whether police work was worth the aftereffects of killing someone as I had done in 'Nam. But I was no longer fighting in a war, I was in my hometown. For the security of my community, because insecurity and distrust intensified for me, I resigned and sought safer employment.

However, a month before I left my position, while on patrol with a training officer in Downtown San José, we got a call for a burglary in progress about a block south of the McDonald's on Third and San Carlos Streets. I took Third Street north and pulled over at the location of the call. Before I knew it, I was back in 'Nam. I looked to my left toward the house and saw a dark backyard area by a carport, alongside a rather high wooden fence at the rear of the house, where two people dressed in black flashed in front of me as they were climbing over the fence. I told my partner about their presence and pointed to the spot.

He said, "there's nothing there!" I felt like warmed over dog poop.

This was not a mistake; it was a hallucination as a consequence of 'Nam, but that was the breakthrough PTSD episode that sealed my fate with police work. For having quit, not only did I get criticized at work, my first spouse would often say.

"Do you think I like being told that you are psycho from Viet 'Nam?"

This event created conflict for me with my co-workers and so-called friends. One of my roommates confided that he was told by others that I didn't make the grade because I wasn't aggressive enough. After that incident that I found a better paying job teaching at CET, and I was suddenly a bachelor again.

Good from bad, I guess.

This new bachelor lifestyle became treacherous for me.

I returned to drinking, just as I did when stationed at Ft. Riley, Kansas after my first tour in 1969. I had about a year left out of my three-year enlistment.

In Kansas, there was absolutely nothing to do. I'd shop at the PX, go to an old gym, check out a basketball, and often I was the only one there for the whole afternoon.

The NCO Club became one of my favorite places to drink. It was inexpensive and the place was well furnished. I had fun there. Only problem was figuring out how to make it back to the barracks. With my military legacy, I soon imagined myself being better off back in 'Nam. Grandpa Ramón and Uncle Fito's alcoholism made me wonder if I too would end up like them, drinking problem and all. I speculated if the historical trauma we carried because of our Native American heritage could be a contributing factor.

ADDICTION AND TRAUMA— WHAT IS THE CONNECTION?

The literature on the science of epigenetics reveals there's no evidence that Native Americans are more biologically susceptible to substance use disorders than any other ethnic group. Native Americans don't metabolize or react to alcohol differently than Whites, and they don't have higher prevalence of any known risk genes within the Native American community. This science links the adversity a person experiences not just to addictions and other mental illnesses, but also to physical disease — including major killers like heart disease, stroke, and diabetes. However, chronic stress matters because elevated levels of stress hormones can suppress the immune system and damage brain cells. These effects abound among Native Americans. Diabetes rates are doubled; liver disease is quintupled. Suicide rates are high. Stressors affect a person's physiology and create auto immune disorders such as diabetes.

The science of epigenetics, literally meaning "above the gene," proposes that we pass along more than DNA; it suggests that we carry memories of trauma experienced by our ancestors that influence the ways we react to them. Essentially, the way genes work in our bodies determines neuroendocrine structures and is strongly influenced by experience. The trauma of earlier generations can influence our genes, making them more likely to "switch on" negative responses to stress and trauma. "Native American healers, medicine people and elders have always known this, and it's common knowledge in Native oral traditions." LeManuel "Lee" Bitsóí is a Navajo PhD in epigenetics who has uncovered that intergenerational reality of trauma. Historical trauma, therefore, is a contributing cause in the development of illnesses such as PTSD, depression, alcoholism, and type 2 diabetes.

I have learned that historical or intergenerational traumas occur in phases. In the initial phase, the dominant culture inflicts mass trauma on a population in the form of colonialism, slavery, war, or genocide. In the second phase the affected population shows physical and psychological symptoms in response to the trauma. In the final phase, the initial population passes it to subsequent generations.

Studies conducted by the National Congress of American Indians (NCAI) have shown that various behaviors and health conditions are inherited epigenetic changes. The research to know more continues. As for me, given this information, it's credible that Grandpa Ramón and his family may link alcoholism and other medical conditions to the Native American Holocaust and racial discrimination, although in my case PTSD is directly related to war.

The war in Vietnam is the source of my pain. It is where the trauma emerges.

THE JUNGLE FIGHTER

Because there were only a few amongst us, I found it difficult to say there were Chicano combat units during the Viet 'Nam War. I was there two years and never saw one. This appears to be a romanticization based on ethnic groups in WW II.

My first tour began March 3, 1968, in a mechanized infantry unit. The group was organized like any other unit, except that it used Armored Personnel Carriers (APCs). Each vehicle transported one squad of up to ten men, with a driver and a gunner and the rest patrolled on foot in the assigned areas. The driver and gunner remained with their vehicles.

My first experience in the field focused on patrolling the Saigon area during the US-Tet counter offensive. I spent about a month as a foot soldier pulling night ambush patrols and Search and Destroy missions. During the day I was an APC driver for about seven months.

It was as a driver that I heard Martin Luther King had been assassinated.

This assignment called for hectic daily driving through the heavy jungle vegetation. At night, I had to pull maintenance on the vehicle and take my turn on guard duty. Most of the time, I slept only three to four hours and sometimes not even that. When I got a chance, I could fall asleep just about anywhere. Sometimes on top of a carboard for the c-rations laid out flat or just on a *pancho*—what we called our rain jackets—spread out on the ground. With these garments, we'd make "hootches," small tent shaped shelters out of two *panchos* snapped together along the edges. One comfort was a blanket called a *pancho* liner. This was

Garcia APC Driver

a rectangular shaped nylon blanket that was insulated and was somewhat water repellent; they warmed us on night ambushes. However, a *pancho* by itself could be noisy at night, and when rain fell on its surface, it made detectable sounds.

Our company pulled land clearing security for large bulldozers called Rome Plows. These plows would tear down very thick jungle vegetation while we protected the troops from attacks. The plows would roll through VC basecamps, and the VC would run out, fire at us or surrender. This went on for months at a time.

In that space, land clearing operations were massive. Huge tree trunks would just crumble into dust with the slightest pressure from an APC. The areas would often show the effects of defoliants. A few times our unit got sprayed by them. We often wondered why there was an oily film on our clothes—it turned out to be Agent Orange which was used on heavy vegetation.

The scariest two areas to which we were mostly assigned were the Iron Triangle and several French rubber plantations. One was the 31,000-acre Michelin Plantation, situated seventy miles northwest of Saigon, halfway between that place and the Cambodian border. The Iron Triangle was a 120 square mile area communist stronghold in the Binh Duong Province in which the Viet Minh had constructed tunnels and fortifications in the 1880's to resist French and Japanese occupations. Whenever we entered that terrain, we knew we'd be "busting jungle" all day long, driving APCs through triple canopy vegetation, and then setting up a night defensive perimeter.

During these maneuvers, I witnessed several guys in my squad get hit by shrapnel. We set up to stop the hits from mortars and rockets that came at night.

One morning in the Triangle, I was next to drive out as lead. We had our patrol route changed and another vehicle took point. It took no more than ten minutes before we heard a blast and large explosion of an anti-personnel mine that was set up at about the height of the vehicle's top surface. Then, we heard the gunner of that vehicle scream.

"My arm. My arm!"

Our medic jumped off from our APC and ran to the guy, pulling down the gunner from the gun turret and onto the vehicle floor, all the while wrapping him up in a *pancho*. We took note of what was left of his right arm and shoulder—bloody mangle of bone and flesh. He screamed all the way to the Medivac Chopper. For each one of us, it was a shockingly close call.

If I close my eyes, I can still see the enormous forests of rubber trees, all lined in perfect rows and columns on flat planes and rolling hills. Each tree held a small ceramic bowl attached with wire, to collect the oozing white milky sap after being slashed with a knife. Local Vietnamese harvested the sap to be coagulated and processed into tire material. The plantation resembled a monstrous fruit tree orchard—it was the ideal theater to conduct fire and maneuver tactics against the North Vietnamese Army (NVA) who were ever-present and ready to battle.

On December 30, 1968, my squad was assigned security detail for a land clearing operation. That morning, my platoon commander Lt. Tucker was told by a helicopter pilot to contact the NVA at a creek. He was told that the enemy was supposed to have surrendered, instead they shot at the pilot. Over the radio Lt. Tucker was told by the pilot, "If you don't go into the stream where the VC are, you'll be relieved of your rank." That's when I took my squad directly into the stream, right into the hands of the NVA who were inside a fortified bunker.

Upon our arrival to the stream bed, about 50 meters from where we were located, we saw a Light Observation Helicopter (LOH) hovering over those who were in the water stream above the NVA. The lieutenant colonel who was commanding the action actively fired his M-16 and dropped fragmentation grenades to the right of the pilot.

My squad entered the stream moving toward the NVA. Our Radio Telephone Operator Specialist Gorham reminded Lt. Tucker of a scheduled 9:15 a.m. situation report to our battalion commander and handed him the radio mike. Lt. Tucker and

Gorham were within arm's reach of each other. The NVA fired on the squad and Gorham was instantly shot and killed and his body sank into the stream under the weight of the radio on his back.

My squad and me opened fire.

Because we were bobbing up and down, we couldn't get Gorham's body out of the stream—we were unable to reach him. The NVA were firing their AK-47's at us and were about fifty meters to the front. My squad then pulled back, about twenty meters from the NVA's location to the stream bed and saw Cobra gunships make rocket and mini gun runs right where Gorham's body was under water. For what appeared to be an eternity, Gorham's body popped up and down in water as we fired at the NVA. Finally, from the splatter of the explosions, Gorham's body bubbled up to the surface.

In their attempt to pull Gorham back, my squad made a second advance into the stream toward the enemy. While firing and maneuvering toward the NVA, I shot one of their soldiers in the head—this was later confirmed by SSgt. Visaya and PFC Dennis Defalco—and the squad advanced. The next day, an APC driver who was at the stream said they pulled Gorham's dead body out when they went back. His body had been stripped of all his clothes and the enemy had taken his weapon and radio.

With those memories ready to surface at any time, sometime in 2012 on a phone call with Lt. Tucker, he admitted to "losing it for a couple of days," and recalled that an after-action report went into Command Headquarters the following day. Our platoon sergeant was briefed at the fire support base, and he recommended US medals for all the squad members. Lt. Tucker set up a field radio antenna for proper reception and called in to our Battalion Commander, Lt. Col. Machenzi. He advised Machenzi about the poor support provided by the pilot the day before, letting him know that our platoon was leaving the operation. We traveled through Bandit Hill to Ben Cat toward a battalion area in the Lai Khe base camp. Tucker told us that he had checked in with the Awards & Decorations unit in Lai Khe but found out that their field office had been rocketed and lost many records.

There were no contact records of that December 30, 1968, day.

It was by mail that I learned that Lt. Tucker had received the Vietnamese Gallantry Cross with Gold Palm in 1970, that the document was in Vietnamese and issued by the Army of the Republic of Viet 'Nam (ARVN). However, those who dispense such recognitions were not present. Gorham was the only 1st squad member to get an American award, although those amongst us who had been injured did not even receive a purple heart. Nonetheless, I thought "I'm not here to get awards. I'm here to defend my country."

In the final analysis, I would pay the price for serving in 'Nam. The rest of my life, I would feel it in my body and soul.

CONSEQUENCES OF WAR

Mid-January 1970 I was hit with the first of two-malaria hospitalizations. My symptoms started like a severe case of the flu, and our medic walked me for an examination at the medical unit. Malaria was confirmed and I was sent to the 93rd Evacuation Hospital in Long Binh. There, I was placed in an open ward and treated with quinine and another medication for parasites in my gut.

To my surprise, the next morning, I saw Larry Lopez, an old neighbor and classmate of mine from East San José. He walked into the ward over to my bed and said,

"Hey Garcia. It's me Larry."

I was able to walk outside to have a chat and smoke a couple joints which seemed to ease the body aches. After three days, I was released to my unit.

A couple of years later, while held at Santa Clara County Jail, I ran into Larry again.

He was serving meals. When he saw me, he gave me an extra dallops.

Earlier that day, in my apartment on North 9th Street, my roommate had come to tell me,

"The cops want you."

There were two officers at the door who came to take me into custody because the municipal court had issued a bench warrant for me to appear. The reason given was that I had applied for and received one unemployment check after being laid off from my night job, while I was a student at San Jose City College. Apparently, as a student I couldn't collect benefits and receive unemployment. For a misdemeanor fraud, I was given probation.

After I met conditions of probation, the matter was cleared from my record.

Memories would take me into other journeys of the mind. Some of these trips took place in Cambodia. However, wherever I found myself, music was always there to soothe my soul.

A NEW BEGINNING

One of my sleepless nights while studying at San José State, I concluded I was captive in a hostile relationship compounded by drug and alcohol abuse. I was fortunate to kick that relationship and rebuild myself through work, study, music performance, and a promising new relationship with the prettiest woman I have ever known.

This was a new beginning. A new start for me.

As a teacher in a local vocational center, I kept busy developing curricula, presenting it to students, and finding them jobs in areas for which they became qualified. This was when I began a period of self-directed landscape irrigation systems design study, and I was now teaching aspects of that to my students and contracting for jobs installing irrigation systems.

It was at this time that my deep appreciation for music took me to study with Latin percussion masters in the Bay Area. I was able to correct old bad habits in my drumming techniques. Much later, in 2013, I studied and performed as a Latin Percussionist at the Capital University Music Conservatory in Bexley, Ohio.

My friend, former band mate and new roommate Phil, and I occasionally rehearsed. We thought we could resurrect *Flor del Pueblo* and make a few bucks gigging in town. Phil's sister, Deborah, brother Pancho, longtime friend Ben and I started meeting and planning performances. After rehearsals, Deborah and I would grab a bite to eat and just talk about our musical experiences.

One time, I was playing with Rudy Madrid and a few guys at Antuna's Taqueria on South 10th Street in San José, and with the hope she'd be there, I had purchased two tickets to the Montalvo

Playhouse. Debbie showed up. I asked her to go with me and she smiled, saying "Yes." For that date, I borrowed my younger brother's nice Oldsmobile Cutlass Supreme and picked her up.

The performance was a murder mystery. It was quite enjoyable.

Through the play, I caught myself looking at the moonlight reflecting off of Debbie's long locks of black hair and smooth skin. I'd never been so close to such a beautiful woman.

Soon, we became closer.

We had some amazing dates and I found myself explaining where my prior poor relationships had taken me. Because of her gentleness I began to feel free to tell Debbie Ann how I felt about her. When we both confessed our love for each other, she told me that I had to love Jesus more than her. I had never heard anyone speak like that. However, our love deepened. I would find out what she meant.

We were married in the Baptist church in which she had been raised and started our journey together, had two daughters, traveled, played music, and purchased a few houses. My Uncle Jose, an old friend of her family from the *huelga* days, repeated a few times, "You're a lucky son of a ^*%&."

My response was always, "I know that Tío."

Change would be the constant in my life. There would be other things that came up for my family and me.

PROBLEMS IN THE HOMEFRONT

In late January 2009, I got a call from my siblings in San José that my 83-year-old father was seriously ill. It was time to fly out and be with my old man—Timoteo Gonzalez Garcia. When I left, my mind was focused on dad's life—he had been my solid foundation. I thought I would do my statistics assignment, but I never did that homework.

On the way, I contemplated on my father's physical strength. He was like no one I knew.

My dad was born and raised in, *La Colonia,* a neighborhood in the coastal town of Oxnard, California. He had to be tough to make it there. He did some of the hardest work a person could do, that of agriculture, in perhaps the roughest Chicano stronghold in Southern California. Memories of my dad framed recollections of my paternal great grandparent's egg ranch in a remote little canyon town by the name of Piru, California, just east of Oxnard and west of Magic Mountain. After migrating from Mexico in 1910, during the revolution, the family settled there and built up a small business selling eggs. They also harvested citrus crops in the area. One of my great-grandparent's sons fought in WW I.

My grandparents were the first family members to live in a farmworker camp on a citrus grove called *La Limoneira*— Portuguese for lemon grove. I visited that place several times and lived there as a child with my parent's when they first got married. My mom said my bed was a fruit crate. Life there was like being in Mexico, as I recall. The way the people looked, what they ate, the music on the radio, roadrunners on the side of the road, people slaughtering their hogs and chickens, and exclusively speaking

Spanish. Some people spoke a mixed code of Spanish and English, but that was about it.

One visit when I was about three years old, a neighbor boy and I decided to climb a hill close to the rear of his and my grandpa's house. We got to the top, and I recall being amazed at the expanse of the orange grove that stretched for miles into the horizon. I would later compare it to the treetops of the French plantation rubber trees configuration in 'Nam and the ways in which the grounds resembled the orange trees of the *Limoneira*.

My friend and I played and stayed close to an irrigation ditch throwing rocks. Soon the neighbor boy decided to jump down onto a concrete pipe that was around a large cast iron canal gate used to direct water to the grove. He got stuck and started struggling to get loose, but he couldn't. He was crying and squirming in the pipe, and I tried to pull him out, but I couldn't. So, I ran down the hill to his house and told his father, the man who had slaughtered a pig the day before. I spoke Spanish, the prevalent language of *La Limoneira's* camp residents, and I was able to convey the problem about his son's predicament, "Your son is stuck." He grabbed a shovel and we both ran back up the hill to where his son was jammed. The man dug around the pipe and loosened it so he could wiggle the boy out.

When we moved to Columbus, Ohio, my dad's house in East San José seemed foreign— the weather was 77 degrees in January, there were very few Black residents, and many Vietnamese, but mainly people of Mexican ancestry who spoke English and Spanish. Ohio was quite different, it had a Southern cultural influence, it snowed quite a bit in winter and the temperature dropped to 15* below zero, and often the wind chill factor could take the temperature below that. This trip to deal with the health emergency of my father allowed me to contrast my change in living situation and it brought countless memories forth.

Although I was raised in an urban setting, a lot of my old neighborhood was like my Grandparents' place. In San José, there were no roadrunners, no hogs, or chickens to slaughter in your backyard for dinner, but the music and language were pretty much the same. There were still plenty of orchards and some close to our house. The eastside of King Road from Shortridge Avenue south had no sidewalks. The corner of San Antonio and King had a small pasture with an occasional cow or horse, and sometimes goats. There would sometimes be signs that hung on the fence reading "Goats 4 Sale."

On my flight back to Ohio, after seeing my dad, I figured his life had been a real miracle. He came out of a very humble upbringing, married my mom, had six kids, and bought two houses—one that's still occupied by my oldest sister and her family—the first house was $8,500.00 dollars which has since appreciated one hundred-fold. For me, my true inheritance was the work ethic I got from my dad, and with that my military service brought honor to our home, despite the fear, exhaustion, and brutality of combat I experienced in Viet 'Nam.

In San José, another legacy I gained were words in the mixed code that my father learned among his contemporary peers who beside being bilingual in English and Spanish, spoke the Pachuco variety of the 1940's. My siblings and I never used it, but we knew what the words meant.

In college I found the vocabulary came from a language referred to as *Caló*, or the Pachuco language of the Southwest—the Mexican Spanish language of the 30's and 40's along the U.S.-Mexico border. A dear family friend, Tony Burciaga, defined Caló as "the Spanish Gypsy dialect." This English Spanish code switching relied on rhythm and rhyme.

Among the many phrases my dad used was *"Nel, pastel."* That translated to "No. I don't think so." There was also *"Al rato vato,"* meaning "Later guy." One very famous Mexican actor,

Tin Tan used *Caló* in the Mexican movies that we saw with my parents at the Liberty Theater on Market close to Post Street. Often, *Caló* words had more than one meaning. For example, "Órale" is used as a salutation, as in "Hello." However, a change in intonation and how it was uttered slowly in a low tone and an extended third syllable made it an expression of approval, like "Okay" or disapproval, as in "Not okay." For my dad shoes were *calcos*, pants were *tramos*, and his house was *mi cantón*.

When he called his brother to tell him Grandpa Claudio Garcia had died, he spoke in the language of the barrio, stating "*Se murió mi jefito.*"

But there is one phrase I will never forget. I heard on that early September day of 1969, before I left home for my second tour in 'Nam. With a grin and a Falstaff beer in his hand, in a tempered scream of desperation, he uttered. "¡Te voy a chingar antes que te vayas!" Or "I'm going to kick your butt before you leave." We were face-to-face when he said it, and I knew he could do it. Instead, he let out joyous laughter because he had gotten my goat.

Pride in my ability to work and my work ethic became my ticket and my superpower when I returned. That's how I secured a job working for the community.

My very first job in San José, after getting out of the Army and taking college classes, was at the Mexican American Community Services Agency (MACSA). Staff at the college job referral desk sent me to the MACSA office located on North 13th Street, right next to Maria's Club—that's where my parents occasionally went to listen to live music with their *compadres*. At MACSA, I interviewed with the Director, Delia Alvarez, a brown woman who asked me about myself. I told her about high school and informed her that I'd just returned from 'Nam. Her response was "You can start tomorrow." When I told my roommate Benny about this, he applied for a job—he had been to 'Nam as a Marine. A few days later, Alvarez hired him. The director was flexible with Benny and me. Soon Benny was doing artwork, and I showed a youth movie series at a community center in the Mayfair area.

After working at MACSA for some weeks, Benny and I learned Delia was an anti-war activist. We also found out that her brother Everett was the longest held POW. I attended some anti-war rallies where Alvarez spoke. The manner in which she balanced her commitment to anti-war activism almost became a personal investment in the war itself. It was remarkable to see how she handled the asymmetrical political and cultural contradictions in our U.S. culture. I figured she had the internalized diplomatic skills to deal with those ambiguities. In 'Nam, I used similar skills when handling racists where nearly everyone was armed. Clearly, it wasn't an easy situation for her, as it was for me in 'Nam.

How she handled her commitment was somewhat like an event I experienced related to a promotion board. I was competing with a few of the other guys, but I thought my awards and decorations and being in my second combat tour would give me the advantage. Well, a white guy in our platoon who had no combat experience and had maybe three months in 'Nam but was a college graduate from Fordham University in New York, and he got the promotion over me. I struggled masking my disgust with the decision, but just pushed the anger to the back of my mind and did what I came to do—remain a fearless jungle fighter. From the border to the center of the nation, I dealt with the demands from home—my parents and all my relations.

In 2010, my paternal side of the family celebrated the 100th anniversary of their arrival to California. Since my family and I had relocated to Ohio, I couldn't attend. Nonetheless, I was proud of this milestone in our family legacy.

This was when, while working for the Ohio Civil Rights Commission as an investigator, I let some of my co-workers know about my heritage. An African American lady in the neighboring office was the first one I told. With a smirk on her face, she said,

"Well, how did they get here? On a donkey?"

I stepped back a few feet as I tried to calm down.

My response was, "On a train. Mexico is an industrialized nation."

Still fuming, on the drive home, the first thing that came to mind was a church song named *"Burrito de Belen,"* which depicts the donkey Jesus rode on Palm Sunday. A few months later, I was out Christmas shopping with my wife and daughters, and I spotted a special tree ornament. It was a multi-colored donkey.

A few weeks after the donkey incident, the woman who made the remark apologized, saying:

"As African American persons, black people can't say where they are from as easily as you can."

Although it had been an enraging situation, one good thing about the "donkey" statement was that it encouraged me to reflect on my family's migratory experience. My paternal family were migrant farmworkers who lived and worked the agricultural fields, and grandfather worked the groves year-round with a company that gave him housing, usually referred to as a farmworker labor camp.

To make ends meet, I learned from my monolingual Spanish-speaking grandmother that she took her eight children, five boys and three girls, to pick crops driving up and down California when the children were not in school. That was sometime in the 1970's, when I asked her, "How did you manage that?" She replied, "We found out about seasonal work from other farmworkers, from growers, and least of all, from a governmental agency. And we usually worked by contract, but, at times, on a piece rate basis."

Grandma had tears in her eyes, as she recalled "we all luckily slept in a tent together," adding "*Sí tenían carpa* or if they even had a tent and many people slept on the ground." They migrated from place to place to sustain themselves.

Like my ancestors, I would walk the farmworker path, and I had my own apricot, green bean, tomato, strawberry, and pear picking experiences during summer breaks. I had a fun time with the guys that I worked with telling jokes and singing rock and roll songs we thought we knew.

One time, a guy named Hector asked me if I liked the song, "Duh-mo-shoo-cook." I asked him "Who sang it." He said, "Elvis, of course." I pondered that title for a while and figured that he meant "I'm All Shook Up." I didn't have the heart to tell Hector and just held back my laughter. When I told the Yankees—the guys in my Mayfair Little League team—we laughed until our tears rolled on the floor.

Our community relationships brought connections.

For example, our league was sponsored by the Pink Elephant Market on King Road, where my dad worked on weekends. That's another way my father paved the way, imparting the importance of hard work and family. A hardworking man, he did the best he could.

Because of my family working legacy, I model his work ethic. Wherever I found myself, I strove to make contributions to the community.

CIVIL SERVANT

My career started as a laborer with the City of San José, working for public works. As a governmental employee, I felt fortunate and altruistic—I served others. After successfully taking a practical test and passing an interview they hired me. Excited to have a job in which I had no layoffs, I had a steady source of income, medical and dental benefits, and access to a credit union. I felt I had it made, even though I did not get paid much. Yet as public servants we were scrutinized as government workers. The public perceived us as lazy.

The work was not easy, and it wasn't free of racial harassment. To begin with, my first supervisor, an Anglo man named Joe Smith, asked me in a morning crew meeting how I got hired? I thought, *"¿Qué pedo? What the f---?* It took me a few seconds to calm down. I scanned the room and looked at the 90 percent Anglo crew and responded, "I got a 95 percent on the test and an received an extra ten points for being a veteran." What a jerk of a boss Joe turned out to be. He assigned me to work with Jack—the bad apple or the oldest maintenance worker on the crew.

Jack had an extremely ravaged face that looked like gravel surface and was the color a neon strawberry. At work, his first stop was a liquor store. Second, he drove to a nearby golf club's snack bar, parked in the shade, and opened his bottle of red wine. I must admit, I had a cup, while Jack kept on drinking until the bottle was empty.

At the end of our shift, we came back to the yard where we kept our vehicles and checked back into our meeting room. It was quiet until Smith asked how it went.

"Pretty good. Jack is a friendly guy."

I knew he wanted me to spill the beans or drop a dime on Jack to get him fired for drinking on the job while driving a city truck. Everybody on the crew saw Jack as a lazy guy waiting to retire after twenty-five years as a city worker.

The next government job I had was as a Police Officer, which only lasted a year. I quit when I came to the realization that I didn't want to kill anybody again. Also, with the stress of the job PTSD symptoms began leaking out. Next, I became a License Registration Examiner for the California Department of Motor Vehicles (DMV) in San José. The job was to give driving tests and issuing licenses.

When I first came in the office for my interview, I looked around at the long lines and thought it looked like the LA Greyhound bus station on a busy day—a memory from 'Nam. The DMV certified me as a bilingual employee and paid me an extra $60.00 dollars per month. In that position, I witnessed several fist fights, deadly weapon assaults, and even one fatal shooting.

There, besides my Vietnamese buddy, the examiners were White females with big attitudes toward Mexicans and Vietnamese. Consequently, these employees failed almost all their ethnic license applicants. In my case, almost all Vietnamese and Mexican applicants passed their driving tests. I think the reason was that I made the applicants feel more at ease, since I conducted the tests in Spanish, and I also could give basic directions in Vietnamese and Cambodian. There, I ran into many old friends trying to get their licenses or helping family members or friends get theirs. I also handled a large amount of monolingual Spanish speakers trying to figure out what to do. I had that job for about two years until I was promoted to hearing officer. That job was quite a switch from just testing. My responsibility was to consider evidence and make a legal determination if a person had the ability to drive safely and then write a report in support of my decisions.

After thirteen years at DMV, I transferred to the California Department of Fair Employment and Housing. I was still rendering decisions based on evidence, however my duties changed to assess whether a person had been discriminated on the job based on their race, age, disability, gender, or sexuality. This was my first exposure to Civil Rights Law enforcement. In that position, I also was certified as a bilingual employee. The best part of the job was securing cash settlements for employees after determining there had been a violation of California laws. On that job, I developed negotiation skills I would take wherever I went.

In 1999, I was hired as a Deputy Labor Commissioner by the California Labor Commissioner's Office. My main duty was to deal with employee complaints when they were not fully paid by an employer.

I had some interesting cases. One was a claim of unpaid overtime for a baker who was employed by the largest Mexican Grocery Store in San José. The facts were clear. The employee had been hired as a baker of *pan dulce*. He supervised no one and had no control over the work or schedules of other employees.

He was directed by his superiors to work over eight-hour shifts to meet production quotas. In this case, the employer acted on the premise that his worker was salaried, and that he was exempt from overtime pay.

In pursuit of this case, other offenses were found. For example, the employer made it his practice to hire undocumented workers for an unpaid two-week trial period. After putting in their two weeks, the worker reported to a supervisor at the store who would decide if they could do the job.

The baker filed a failure to pay overtime complaint and submitted his record of overtime hours. The evidence showed that he was not exempt from overtime. In his words, he was just a baker, "*un simple panadero.*"

When the local mercantile workers union learned of the grocer's illegal practices, union representatives convinced several store employees to picket the store. In subsequent interviews with the employee, the worker told me of the troubles store picketers were having. The owner went as far as having his accountant intimidate the picketers with his trained attack dogs. Given the situation, the commission allowed me to read a script of those practices for Spanish television. After the Telemundo crew reported these illegal activities, this particular complaint was resolved, and the worker agreed to a settlement equal to the unpaid overtime and the waiting time penalty for the worker's daily rate of pay. When the *panadero* came in to pick up his check, he told me he was returning to his home village in Mexico and would retire a wealthy man.

The most awkward case I handled was against the United Farm Workers (UFW)—it was submitted by a woman for unpaid overtime. Her job involved contacting farmworkers in her community who wanted information on the union, and she organized meetings at their homes. She kept records of her hours.

In analyzing the information provided, I determined she wasn't exempt from overtime laws and was due several unpaid hours, plus a penalty equal to her daily rate up to thirty days. Some of my co-workers were former UFW members who gave me grief about my determination of unpaid overtime. The UFW attorney was unable to refute my recommendation and cut a check for the full amount.

Undocumented workers would also seek my services. They too had workers' rights.

In June 2007, while employed by the Ohio Civil Rights Commission, I took a complaint from a Honduran-born female employee of a large Mexican grill chain store in Columbus. I received a call from Ohio Catholic Social Services about what the employee had explained to them. In turn, they filed a discrimination complaint that her White male supervisor sexually assaulted her several times, after locking the bathroom door while she had been cleaning. He told her that she couldn't do anything about it because she was "illegal." After the company was notified, the supervisor was warned but later promoted to a position in another state.

The attorney for the Tex-Mex restaurant agreed to settle the claim. When I notified the employee about the offer, per my recommendation we asked for more.

The worker returned to her village in Honduras to comfortably retire.

RAZA RAPTURE

In 2022, I finally visited the Vietnam War Memorial. The Wall in Washington, DC tallied six Richard Garcias.

I often thought how lucky I was to survive the war and wondered why so many of us went to 'Nam. In fact, a study written in 1979 by Ralph Guzman from Cal State Los Angeles found that Latinos totaled 20 percent off all U.S. troops killed in Vietnam. Another study showed that 178,000 Hispanics served in 'Nam and 3,070 died.

Other than being drafted, why did Chicanos go to Vietnam?

In my case, it wasn't solely based on the desire to gain access to resources otherwise not available. Also, there was a part of me that wanted to be accepted as an American fighting man. Like most kids in my neighborhood age group, I was immersed in Audie Murphy movies—who was rumored to be of Mexican-descent—at the Mayfair Theater. He was portrayed as a hero like the one we thought we could become to be accepted by the dominant culture.

The likelihood of becoming a hero like Audie or a family member who fought in a U.S. war created overwhelming emotions. This resembled mystical encounters in which one is spiritually ascended to social acceptance—*raza* rapture. The Bible addresses the Rapture as part of God's redemptive plan to restore what was lost in Adam.

So, that is my take on why I decided to serve in 'Nam—my chances of being accepted by the dominant culture, presuming military service could restore that loss. As many others had, I shared this patriotic trance with which I would contend the rest of my life. In a secondary way, serving in Vietnam would

Squad Member Alan Acosta

positively impact me and those whom I loved for the rest of our lives. I didn't account for the negative consequences that would come with the experience.

THE SPIRIT IN VIET 'NAM

Around April of 1968, an awareness of my spirit was awakened by Francis "Luck" Luckangelo, a good Italian Catholic boy from South Philadelphia. He was a dear friend, plus we went through training and got our orders together.

We were assigned to the same infantry platoon. I have no other way to describe the insight I gained in a base camp on Highway 13, the infamous Thunder Road which ran north to the Cambodian border. Our assignment was to walk point and provide backup for the company. He said, picking up his M-16 and web gear.

"Richard. Pray with me now!"

I responded, "Okay, Luck." And I did the same.

After adjusting our gear, he shouted at the top of his lungs.

"Lord, if you say this is my day to die, I am ready now!"

Every morning that was our prayer and I internalized this utterance by speaking it softly to myself. It became my daily ritual during two tours—with my mechanized infantry company and the Aero Rifle Platoon. This practice prepared me to deal with what came our way. It also activated my adrenaline flow for the mission's requirement of ultra-alertness.

RACIALLY MOTIVATED JURISPRUDENCE

My tours in 'Nam prepared me to deal with conflict and odd circumstances. Prior to my occupation as an Ohio Civil Rights Commission Bilingual Investigator, I was involved in the examination of civil rights violations, focusing on state claims with monolingual Spanish speakers.

Mondays often brought forth negative feelings and thoughts. One Monday in August I brought a case for discussion to a regularly schedule staff meeting. The case was one in which a Mexican gentleman was fired from his job of about five years. The employer's position was that the worker was terminated because he told them that he was undocumented. The worker denied it and added that the boss knew of his status the entire time he was employed and brought documentary evidence. This was not an unusual case.

At this meeting, the Ohio Assistant Attorney General claimed that worker was an "illegal alien" who couldn't claim back pay because of the controlling court case in this issue. To support his case, he cited Hoffman Plastic Compounds, Inc. v. NLRB (2002) 535 U.S. 137 without realizing that the Supreme Court held that although Hoffman violated the National Labor Relations Board (NLRB), claiming that the discharged employee wasn't owed back pay because he had violated immigration laws and shouldn't have had the job.

Why would a law be drafted to show that undocumented immigrants have no civil rights in this country?

My biggest question was why would employers use the immigration status of an employee to relieve themselves of the responsibility of paying mandated overtime? More questions would surface in redressing the rights of workers that could readily be dismissed because of race, ethnicity, and immigrations status. These types of legal maneuvers were not issues with which I had to contend. In 'Nam ethnic people in war played similar parts.

CAMBODIAN INVASIONS

A month prior to the US Cambodian Invasion of late April 1970, my squad was assigned a dark brown fourteen-year-old Cambodian mercenary named Lee; he would act as a scout and interpreted for us. That's how I got to know him. Lee laughed like a teenager but smoked and drank like a grown man and was a fierce fighter in the field. He was very strong for someone 5'6" tall who weighed about 125 pounds. He could carry a heavier load than most guys in the squad.

One afternoon, while we were waiting for a mission, he took off his talisman and in Lee's best English he explained its meaning to me. He laid out a dark green scarf on a table and placed three small balls of what looked like clay marbles. The scarf had what appeared to be Sanskrit writing and had an illustration on it. Lee believed that the balls were his parent's brains—a Cambodian ancestral worship.

On April 29, 1970, my group was flown to a village named Snoul just on the other side of the Cambodian-Vietnam border. The day before, Lee had informed me, "We go Cam-bod." He seemed to know why he was sent to us. During that briefing, we were shown an area on a map in the shape of a fishhook. We were flown due west of our base of Loc Ninh just a few minutes away. On board the Huey helicopter, I noticed my *carnal* brother-in-arms Specialist Julian Castro had a Styrofoam cup of coffee. Castro was a dark brown Chicano from Corona, California. He had his own collection of Oldies but Goodies eight track tapes in his quarters. He was about 5'6" and was exceptionally strong and had the look of a scar-faced pirate.

After landing, we walked across a bridge the NVA had blown up as they fled west, away from the invading US military. Shortly after that, we were flown to a French Villa and waited on their airfield. A small airplane landed, and an old black French sedan

Mercenary Scout Lee

pulled up to it and the French plantation owners boarded the plane, as if there was no war—just a simple business flight.

We continued to patrol the area and found several hidden weapon caches and some abandoned cargo trucks along paved and unpaved roads. A day or two after that, we pulled a daytime ambush along a trail in the area.

While walking point to the site, the silence was deeply familiar. Whistling sounds caused by the friction of my pants and my shirt, as we walked through the elephant grass, were also amplified. With each footstep the sounds became more pronounced.

That ambush resulted in two deaths. We also found several useful documents.

When we were done, we were instructed to quickly leave the area and went to a nearby river, got into it, and arrived at our extraction zone, where we'd get our flight back to base. I wasn't too surprised by the operation since we conducted cross border missions frequently. The next day, we received a call to secure a helicopter crash site.

We landed in an open grass field and headed a short distance into the forest. There, we saw a burned-out helicopter with the remains of its crew still belted unto their seats. We were given large plastic body bags into which we placed the badly burned bodies and took them on board a medivac helicopter.

Once we finished the cleaning operation, we headed to the open field where we had landed earlier and returned to the base. In the air, once we leveled off, we took fire from a heavy machine gun, like the one in which Jane Fonda took a picture. A minute later, I saw a large fireball left by a jet fighter that crashed into one of the Cobra Gunships covering for us.

Back at the base, we settled down and were debriefed on the events of the day. No worries. We had learned how to mellow out in this madness. Even if we had to rely on chemicals to change our everyday reality. My friend and I had scored some opium laced weed. We smoked some in one of my well-seasoned Dr. Grabow pipes purchased at the PX.

Squad Members Garcia and Castro

The sensation from the small black bits of opium left us with crystal clear eyesight, along with the hallucinogenic effects of the weed—that was the medicine that provided me relief from the stress of the day. It worked so well I snuck some of it and mailed it to San Jo, by shipping two softball sized sacks of weed into some stereo speakers I sent home in a footlocker. Once I returned home, my brother took me to my stash.

The conflicts of war demarcate the legal and moral realities we experienced, changing the very meaning of combat. This is a source of survivor's guilt that's best described in a message from one of my squad members while with the ARPs. James spoke about how he and John were wounded:

It's March 15, 1970. Deep into Cambodia. A highly defensive North Vietnamese Gorilla Base camp where thirty-three north Vietnamese died and about seventy were wounded and every Aero Rifle Platoon (ARP) member was protected when Sgt. Prattas entered the base camp first because, with only twelve days left in the country, he had to make the leadership decision to walk point himself. Sgt. Garcia was on R&R, and we had three new men. Sgt. Prattas was awarded a Bronze Star and Purple Heart for sacrificing himself to save the team. A 50 caliber round went through him. No one other than me were at this mission. Other leaders showed up three hours later and the battle was still happening. I believe that was the largest Aero Rifle Platoon-Long mission with the highest number of enemies killed—over thirty-three.

I was not part of that operation because James and John had convinced me to take a three day leave to Vung Tau, a coastal resort south of Saigon. I recall that when I was about to depart, my buddies handed me $100.00 dollars, and they saw me off to our airstrip, where I boarded a Caribou cargo plane to my destination. There, I was assigned to a nice room with a large fan above a bed with sheets and a clean private shower, I had a relaxing time.

Being clean was quite a luxury for a combat soldier.

At the resort, I rented a horse drawn carriage and went sightseeing along the beach, where I saw a huge white statue of Buddha, and walked to the top of the peak in the bay. I had steak dinners every night and breakfast of ham and eggs by a pool. I was the Chicano James Bond who remembered to pack his .45 pistol for the trip. For me, not carrying a weapon was like being in one of those dreams where you see yourself naked in a crowd—exposed!

When the three-day leave was over, I flew back to the Quon Loi Base Camp. I walked to my area and asked for James and John and was told "they were severely wounded the day before."

The guilt I felt was choking me. They had taken my place leading the squad with whom we walked point.

A few days later I came down with a second case of malaria. This time, I really thought I would die. But I was healed from the disease.

I've had a few relapses. However, I'm fortunate enough to have my wife Debora near who watches closely over me.

Back to Quon Loi

MY DAD IS GONE!

In late January 2009, my siblings called to tell me that my 83-year-old father was seriously ill. Now it was time to fly out and be with my old man Timoteo Gonzalez Garcia.

For the duration of my trip, I had flashbacks about how physically strong he was. Memories of my dad framed recollections of my paternal great-grandparents' egg ranch. That was where they settled and built a small business. However, the most unpleasant memory of those times was about that man who dug around a pipe to wiggle his boy out of a canal.

This trip back to deal with the health emergency of my father had me reflect on my past. Although raised in an urban setting, much of my old neighborhood was like my Grandparents' place. These memories have remained with me forever. Even when I've moved far away from home, I carry them inside me.

In my work as an investigator at the Ohio Rights Commission, I proudly told my co-workers about the one-hundred-year anniversary of my paternal family's migration to California. They were migrant farmworkers who lived and worked on a large citrus farm, and grandfather worked the groves year-round when the family lived in a farmworker labor camp. Another story I recall from my monolingual Spanish-speaking grandmother re-surfaced about those times she took her eight children, five boys and three girls, to pick crops driving up and down California, when the children were not in school.

Our community interactions and relationships brought connections for us, even in the agricultural fields. That's how I learned the most important lesson—the value of work an example provided by my dad. He was the hardest working man I knew.

SPIRITUAL AND MORAL INJURIES

My Army Basic Training involved physical combat training and testing. On a few occasions, while on the rifle range located in White Sands, New Mexico, I witnessed surface to air missiles being tested.

I was raised "a good Catholic boy" who attended Our Lady of Guadalupe Church in East San José during the 1950s and 1960s. The church practiced a Catholic influence passed down from prior Mexican generations.

Before the horrors of Vietnam, I was spiritual person who strongly believed in God. As a child I was instructed with the Ten Commandments, beginning with "thou shall not kill." As a young adult while at war, I confronted many religious contradictions.

During the Vietnam War, Catholic churches found themselves between the political turmoil of the 1960s and their theological convictions.

After several battles, I attended many solemn Catholic assemblies in the field. I don't recall the priests addressing the purpose of war or whether killing was sinful. We usually prayed for the souls of fellow soldiers, so that those who were killed in battle would rest in peace for eternity. Well, what else was there?

One significant Catholic moral authority I relied on was St. Thomas Aquinas. His just war theory had a lasting impact on the Catholic church through his detailed reflections on peace and war. He contemplated these biblical teachings in combination with ideas from Aristotle and other philosophers. In *Summa Theologica*, Aquinas asserts that it's not always a sin to wage war and set out the three criteria for a just one. First, the war must be waged upon the command of the rightful and highest of leaders. Second, the war needs to be waged for a just cause being on account of some committed wrong. Third, warriors must have the right intent which means to promote good and avoid evil. He therefore concluded that a just war could be offensive, and that injustice should not be tolerated to avoid war. However, Aquinas argued that violence must only be a last resort.

On the battlefield, violence was only justified to the extent necessary. Soldiers needed to avoid cruelty and a just war was limited by the conduct of just combatants. Aquinas argued that it was only in the pursuit of justice, that the good intention of a moral act could justify negative consequences, including the killing of the innocent. Weapons such as napalm, white phosphorous and the killing of South Vietnamese civilians caused a personal spiritual contradiction for me. I, as most Catholic soldiers, were instructed to honor a strict adherence to the Ten Commandments.

I am sure I wasn't the only one. Catholic priests in 'Nam confronted similar inconsistencies in this regard. But they were expected to represent God despite moral contradiction. If I, as a lay Catholic person had this moral-religious contradiction, priests must've had the same thoughts as they interpreted the scriptures to soldiers within a wartime context.

Based upon the just war philosophy, I received interpretations of scripture and messages on faith from Catholic chaplains that contradicted what both they and I had learned in childhood. I saw this as a source of tension between the official stance of the church, my personal convictions, and experiences with chaplains during the war. This was a moral injury or guilt resulting from breaking of my personal moral code, as I could not compartmentalize the killing of other human beings who were my equal.

As a child, I was taught that killing was a mortal sin. I still carry those beliefs, although I have come to recognize the contradiction in life—it's about birth and death.

MAIL CALL . . .

October of 2022, I had the good fortune of participating in an Honor Flight Tour of the Washington DC Memorials. Honor Flight is a non-profit organization that arranges all expenses paid trips for veterans to visit war memorials. As my guardian, my oldest daughter accompanied me—it was expected that she would attend to our needs during the tour. She was splendid.

A month prior to the tour, an orientation was held at the local Veterans of Foreign Wars (VFW) Hall. Those who were selected attended with their designated guardians. The first thing on the agenda was to provide an explanation of the tour's purpose, and to detail expectations for the veterans and their guardians. At the conclusion of the orientation, we were provided a t-shirt, a windbreaker, and a travel bag with the logo of Honor Flight, along with a nametag to wear.

Next, the veteran and their guardian were instructed to provide a two-minute introduction. One of the veterans, a former Army Captain who served as a nurse between 1969 and 1971 at the 93rd Evacuation Hospital in Long Binh, looked familiar to me.

When introductions ended, I approached the former nurse captain. Told her I had been medevac'd to that hospital for treatment of malaria in late 1969. She told me that I had been her patient because she oversaw the nurses in that facility.

All I could say was, "Well, then. You saved my life."

The army captain let out a scream and gave me a hug and kissed my cheek.

In DC, we renewed our acquaintance and spoke about that time together as if it had been yesterday. During an open mic session

Viet 'Nam Memorial

at one of our dinners, I addressed the group and told them about this wonderful person I had met fifty-three years ago. I expressed that "if it had not been for her care, my daughter and I would not be at the celebration."

Later that night, my daughter said, "much has been revealed about you." She had heard me explain how I had been affected by Agent Orange, a symptom which is part of my VA disability rating. Just ten feet away from me, she heard me speak to the group about the ways in which four guys in my squad had been killed on the same date.

The secrets of war I had been stuffing came out. I had never shared any of this with my children before. She learned about these and other experiences in my conversations with the veterans.

At the gathering, my daughter spoke about me as the father who was always working, going to school, or serving in the Marine Reserve. She told the audience about our paternal side of the family and that we had lived in a lemon grove camp surviving in abject poverty. In her aim to illustrate how far we had come as a family, she shared that my first bed had been a lemon crate. The ways in which PTSD and other war afflictions keep me connected to the past gives me hope for the future, my loved ones, and me.

An interesting part of the program was "Mail Call." This exercise was done to illustrate the importance of family communications with those in the U.S. military. The process entailed calling each veteran's name and presenting them with a packet of letters collected by volunteers from various organizations.

Three special letters were in my packet. One from my youngest brother David and one each from my sisters—Caroline and Elaine—describing how the war had affected them and my parents. My siblings wrote about their inability to understand why their oldest brother went to war. My parents merely told them I was serving our country and expressed the importance of prayer for my safe return. They wrote that mother was severely saddened by the situation and that our father was nervous about the war and vigilantly watched the news for updates.

On a regular basis, my family and I wrote to each other. They described family holiday celebrations and birthdays in those letters. They also sent me large boxes of canned goods and sweets. That was a special occasion for me, and I shared what I received with my squad.

Sometime around my twentieth birthday, I sent my family a photo of me, with a three-year-old Vietnamese baby girl named Mai. She and her family lived under the Song Be River Bridge. Her father was a South Vietnamese soldier assigned to guard the bridge and we were there to assist. When mom received the photo, she sent me a gift box containing a fancy pink dress and a doll for Mai. When I was leaving the area, I gave the gifts to Mai's mother who was overjoyed with such a pretty dress and doll from America. My platoon and I were delighted to see Mai and her mother's huge smiles and the shouts of "thank you."

Interestingly, that war did not take away the joy that came from dreams of home and family love. I often wonder how others, besides the service members killed or wounded in Viet 'Nam, endured war. I have relatives who were students and got draft deferments. One was in the service but was medically discharged because of an emotional illness. Another obtained a deferment with a divinity diploma based on religious convictions. I often wondered how administrators—the decision makers who promoted the escalation of war—dealt with those requests. Even though he probably knew the war was unwinnable, Secretary of State McNamara made grave decisions.

As I continue to learn about the war no one spoke about, there is one American I have learned about, Norman Morrison, who was a Quaker from Baltimore. At the age of thirty-one, he committed the act of self-immolation to protest United States involvement in the Vietnam War. He was married and had two daughters and a son. On November 2, 1965, during rush hour, while thousands of American draft deferred students were adjusting to the rigors

Richard and Mai

of their studies, Morrison doused himself in kerosene and set himself on fire below Robert McNamara's Pentagon office, with his infant daughter by his side.

This action taken mirrored the act of Thich Quang Duc and other Buddhist monks, who burned themselves to death, to protest the repression committed by Catholic President Ngo Dinh Diem of the South Vietnam government. Seven days after Morrison's death, at sunrise, in front of the United Nations building, a twenty-two-year-old Catholic named Roger LaPorte set himself on fire. There were others who took stands against the war.

My journalist hero because of that aura of being a Chicano movement martyr, Ruben Salazar, was a civil rights activist and a reporter for the Los Angeles Times. The first Mexican American journalist from mainstream media to cover the Chicano community, Salazar wrote several columns in support of activists opposed to the Vietnam War.

During a march, which he was there to report, Ruben Salazar was struck and killed by a tear gas projectile fired by Los Angeles County Sheriff's Deputy Thomas Wilson. Salazar's body remained on the floor of the Silver Dollar Bar, the location where he was shot, for nearly three hours when a pair of homicide detectives from the Los Angeles County Sheriff's Department finally arrived to examine the body. Reports show they noted the button pinned to his jacket: "Chicano Moratorium. 8,000 Dead. ¡Ya Basta! [Enough Already!]" No criminal charges were filed for his death, but his family reached an out-of-court financial settlement with the county. Even in death Salazar's corpus of work continues to proclaim his solidarity with their cause.

Memories about families are integral in the reclamation of whom we are and become. I dearly appreciate these memories. To remind me of those from whom I descend, these recollections flow in and out of my mind—they give me life. Inspire me to go on.

When I was about eight years old, my family and I took my dad's mom for a ride through the orange groves of Ventura County. My brother and I rode in the back seat with mom. Grandma and dad were in the front while he drove our still shiny green '51 Chevy Deluxe coupe. We stopped at a local *campesino* hamburger spot in a small town named Saticoy. This burger joint was shaped like a giant orange. We ordered hamburgers and sat there enjoying them. I remember asking Grandma what she called hamburgers in Spanish. She looked back at me and my brother and said, "am-bur-gue-sa." My brother and I cracked up and asked her to repeat it. She did. Her response sounded like boogers to us. Since she was a very stoic religious Methodist woman, grandma smiled back at us which was a big deal.

Whenever grandma left the house, she wore a bandana and a long dress. After my grandpa died, she wore the same thing, only in black. During a month's leave, prior to starting my second tour at 'Nam, I went to visit grandma in her new home in *La Colonia*. My aunt Maria and uncle Benny were there, and tío told my aunt not to tell grandma I was going back to "Ventura," his code word for Viet 'Nam.

Several years later, my wife Debora pointed out that my Army picture was the only one on grandma's mantle. In those visits I had with her, we truly connected. Later, she moved to the East LA's City Terrace area, on Bonnie Beach Drive, above Hazard Park. I played basketball with some older neighborhood kids. I was thirteen and had played a lot of basketball at my Roosevelt Jr. High's gym—it was after school and on Friday nights. I walked there and back from King Road and San Fernando, feeling safe in my neighborhood, which has changed to the point that I wouldn't walk the streets now as an adult.

At that time—about the fall of 1970—I was brooding because of a Dear John letter I'd received some months back. I now see it as a great favor.

One day I was waiting at my parents' house for a friend who was a San José State Chicano activist, to attend a Coors Boycott Committee meeting, when our conversation turned to the letter I received, which he claimed generated obvious signs of depression. Also, with the gift of discernment, my mother gave me and the entire family insight into our relationships. She told my friend that she had warned me, "About that girl." She had expressed extreme reservations about her. My friend confirmed it when he said, "Yeah, when you were gone, she was messing around with my brother for a few years."

I dealt with the loss through lonely pot smoke-filled nights of driving around in my blue VW bug, blasting *Santana* and *El Chicano* on my 8-track stereo all around East San José. I was not a participant or a believer of the widespread free love culture happening at that time.

When I reflect on 'Nam, a particular incident surfaces to the top. It is those moment that expose our limitations, failures, frustrations, and disappointments—and therefore our secrets and vulnerabilities—and take us back to fundamental fear.

In my experience with the 11th Cavalry Aero Rifle Platoon, I feared killing another person even more than dying. On or about March 1970, I was the point man on a daytime ambush with the ARPs. I know it happened before the Cambodian invasion because Lt. Douglas P. Rich was my platoon leader, and he is a marker in the calendar for that time.

A time that is memorable for two reasons. First, the regimental commander, Col. Starry was with us. He was the only guy wearing a flak jacket and steel-pot. The second? Well, read on.

As with many missions, we boarded our Hueys at Quon Loi Base, and not very early one morning we headed toward Cambodia. It took us about an hour to reach our landing zone and to secure the insertion area as soon as our helicopters lifted off. Finally, we made our way into the wood line of triple canopy jungle. We took compass azimuth north in the celestial sky—toward the area where we were to set up an ambush. It was along a walking trail which had rectangular dug-in positions alongside both sides of the trail, each about 6' x 6' x 3' deep. This was just enough cover and concealment for the ambush. We set out antipersonnel claymore mines and settled in, quietly along the trail.

ARP Insertion

There were about a dozen ARPs plus Lt. Colonel Starry and his aide. About an hour went by with no movement. Suddenly from my sniper's position ten feet to my left I heard the click boom of a claymore mine exploding and the *pop-pop-pop* from an M-14 sniper rifle. When we checked the trail, we found two wounded individuals moaning from their injuries. They were both dressed in Vietnamese civilian clothes. A trail of blood led away from the path. Colonel Starry checked the wounded enemy soldiers out and declared, "Infiltrators."

Lt. Rich asked, "Do you want to walk point after the blood trail or let Sniper Specialist Mackey take it." Walking point is a strange out of body experience. Your senses are fully awakened, and you can hear each blade of elephant grass whistle as it rubs across your clothing and weapon.

"Let Mackey do it," I said. "He shot the other guys."

Lt. Rich looked back at the trail and the two severely wounded people.

"Do what you got to do, then throw the bodies in the emplacements."

One of the bodies was still alive when I pulled my Air Force survival knife. While the imagery is still somewhat foggy, there are times I've come to the realization that I stabbed him, before rolling him into the emplacements. That daytime ambush in early May 1970 in Cambodia, dressed in a soldiers uniform, I was the butcher reflecting that early childhood of killing a pig for our feast and the memory I carry about killing an NVA soldier.

Although he resisted and squirmed, trying to break my hold on him, he did not cry out when I stabbed him in the neck with my military issued survival knife designed for such action. Unlike the pig slaughtered at the *Limoneira*, the NVA soldier did not cry out or scream, probably due to high state of shock due to severe injuries from claymore anti-personnel mines.

Like the butcher that had mounted that pig, when I approached the prone NVA soldier, he gazed at me with a stunned stare, looking away as if to find an escape from my grasp. Still, he tried to crawl away from me until I put my weight on his elbows with my knees to hold him still. Then, he began to resist, convulsing slightly but moaning loudly, as if to give our position away to his nearby comrades. He gazed at me with a stunned stare and looked away. The fatal wounding took a second, from knife sheath to the bony portions of the front of his neck. The smell of the dirt on the trail where I held the soldier down was similar to that of *Limoneira* dirt, as well, and the scent of soldier's blood resembled that of the pig. Yet, unlike the pig slaughtered at the *Limoneira*, the NVA soldier did not cry out. Back at the camp, my squad would celebrate the results of our event over hot chow, cold beer, and weed.

Years later at a reunion, Mackey asked me,

"Do you remember what you did?"

I told him "I wasn't too sure, but that dying soldier has resided in my mind since then."

How is that possible?

When I went back to the States, I reflected. The Vietnamese are, for the most part, Buddhist. In the Vietnamese culture, ghosts are believed to be wandering souls who impact the daily lives of Vietnamese people. Ghosts are known as *ma, hồn, vong, hồn ma, bóng ma, linh hồn, vong hồn, oan hồn, bách linh*—each one represents the many expressions of spirits on earth. They can be pleasant and fearful, harmless, and dangerous, moral creatures and unhappy suicides, male and female, human and non-human. Certain ghosts are people who died unnatural, premature, painful, or violent deaths, especially when those people died away from home. This differs from ancestors who died a good death in their homes with the proper rituals in place.

In Vietnam, souls are understood to need certain items in the afterlife. Souls must receive the proper rituals, have burial in a good location with a proper tombstone. The departed will be nourished by the family, and they will reciprocate by helping the family and its members prosper. Those who don't receive such treatment become ghosts and roam the countryside stealing what they can along the way. "Hungry ghosts" are called *ma doi*.

Belief in ghosts influenced the ways in which Vietnamese dealt with North Vietnamese soldiers who didn't receive proper burials in their home communities. As a result, ghosts of the soldiers are said to wander these areas and there is now a great desire among the Vietnamese to discover where the remains of the deceased are located, to bring them home to their villages for reburial.

Despite psychotherapy and medication at the V.A., these hungry ghosts have followed me. Emotional triggers have emerged to cause me to examine the moment of my greatest fear and I now understand it.

Like the hungry ghosts, my soul must be unearthed, brought home, and reburied with proper ritual and monument so my tablet can be installed in the altar of my family's ancestors.

There, my beloveds may nourish me, and I can prosper and protect them.

THE SPIRIT OF QUON LOI

Quon Loi has its own spirit. I say this because of many unexplained experiences I've had. We often have heard accounts of loved ones who, though the miles separate them, suddenly wake from a sound sleep, aware that a husband, wife, relative or friend is in danger. Only later do they learn more fully what occurred at that precise moment. This phenomenon is unexplained.

There is a realm that transcends our physical senses. Communication in the spirit realm does not depend upon the spoken word; instead, we perceive it with our thoughts. Jesus Christ said, "the wind bloweth where it listeth, and thou hearest the sound thereof, but canst not tell whence it cometh and whither it goeth: so is every one that is born of the Spirit" (John 3:8).

Let me elaborate. In 1980, I went to the Wine Country in California for a little vacation, to get away with my wife. We had great food and wine, and best of all, we had a mud bath. If you have ever had one, you know how limp your body gets. You become extremely relaxed.

After showering off, you go to a room and you get wrapped in a blanket, to drain the toxins. There I was, on my back facing a large ceiling fan, turning just slow enough to provide a slight breeze on my face.

While tending to my well-being, I daydreamed about 'Nam, and imagined the Huey blades again, re-experiencing the Vung Tau trip, my guys getting shot, and my stay at II Field Force Hospital. I wondered if I should get up or just ride it out. I rode it out as I had done a few other times, examining how it would have been for me if John and James hadn't insisted, I go

Richard and His Squad

to Vung Tau. I would finally publicly share my life with these two soldiers.

At a reunion in Kentucky several years ago, I explained my relationship with John and James and that incident in detail. However, even today I wonder how things would have turned out had I been there.

I am thankful to have people in my life who embrace me as I am. Wounds and all.

MUSIC IS LIFE AND LIFE IS EMPTY WITHOUT MUSIC

Ben Cadena has been such a person in my life. Best of all because we share the gift of creativity in music. I will always be thankful for Ben who has been my friend since the seventh grade. Music has brought us together.

Ben played with musicians who would become my family members before I met them in 1970. My wife and brothers-in-law often repeat the statement made by Ben, in association with his love for music. "Music is my trip."

Music is also one of my loves.

This musical journey I've taken with Ben still continues. I also learned from others around us, such as my teacher, Mr. Hauser, at Roosevelt Jr. High who taught me the *danzón* pattern, the *cinquillo* and the *baqueteo* in half-hour sessions in our school music room.

At my one of our concerts, I recall a Chicano family looking at me quite intently, as they listened and seemed to have been taken up by the rhythm, when I played a short version of the *paseo*, Spanish for the *danzón* introduction. The *danzón* rhythm is accomplished in two parts: Cinquillo and *baqueteo*. A *cinquillo* is a traditional rhythmic cell used in Cuban *danzón*. The pattern consists of an eighth, a sixteenth, an eighth, a sixteenth, and an eighth note. It is followed by a *cinquillo* consisting of four unsyncopated eighth notes—the whole pattern is called *baqueteo*.

Between ages eleven to fourteen I played with the Roosevelt marching band, and it was a lot of fun and had many practices for local parades. Later, I played with a few local Mexican bands and was seduced by the *timbales* as my instrument of choice. Because

I was in high school, I missed the walkout for an inclusive and equal education staged at Roosevelt Junior High School, but I saw Sofia Mendoza and other adults lead the walkout in that middle school. Although few have written about it, that was the first walkout for educational rights in the nation—my middle school and San José, California, hold that distinction.

When I returned from 'Nam, I went to see my friend and neighbor Ben Cadena who had played with numerous local bands and mariachi groups. When I asked Ben what he had been up to in the last three years, he made the infectious statement, which has become his motto, "Music is my trip."

Ben and I were known for barrowing school instruments for weekend practices at home. A memory I've kept is that one when Ben and I were walking home from Roosevelt Jr. High, in the fall of 1960. I checked out a 14" calf head wooden snare drum with real cat gut snares, and Ben checked out a sousaphone.

That sunny day, we rode the bus to get home. The bus pulled over, and stepping unto the bus, I imagined Ray Charles whom the driver looked like as the driver. I got in and put my token in the bus fare box, while Ben squeezed in his humongous instrument. The driver looked at Ben and said, "It's a good thing you don't play the piano." That was before we played with the Flores Brothers Band—Andy, Tommy, and Monico. Ben has always been a talented musician. He performed various genres and played with numerous Chicano, jazz, and salsa groups.

Since the early years of our friendship, he has hooked up me with several groups. Some were excellent. Other not so much.

For many years, Ben and I played with Rudy Madrid a San José musician and composer beloved by locals who love music. For several years we also played with *Trio Intimo* and *Flor Del Pueblo*.

I'll never forget the negative experience I had with one of his band hookups that went from bad to worse. He told me about a salsa band that rehearsed in South San Francisco. I got the address and showed up for rehearsal. All was going fine until the male leader showed up in a bikini. I was extremely uncomfortable with this situation but made it through the rehearsal. At the end, the group was told that they were booked at a club in San Francisco called *The Ramp*. I called Ben the next day and said, "Thanks a lot!" Ben just laughed and said he was just kidding around with me to see my reaction. I called the leader the next day and let him know I could not make the gig. He asked, "Why not?" All I could say was "I have some family matters to deal with." He probably believed I declined the invitation to perform because of discomfort.

Throughout our musical trajectory, Ben and I played several funerals together. Both of my parents and my in-laws' services. One of the many *Flor Del Pueblo* funeral services was in Morgan Hill for a family member. The funeral home was next to its own casket sales showroom, and next door was where we practiced for the service.

Also, Ben and I accompanied Danny Valdez. This gig included several live performances and a few recording sessions.

One significant performance was accompanying Danny on bongo for César Chávez's funeral service. Those in attendance, included several Hollywood stars, the Kennedy family,

Jesse Jackson, Willie Brown, and UFW dignitaries. After we finished our set, a member of an LA group called *Los Perros* asked me to back up Jesse Jackson on drum. I agreed, and since I had not played drums in several years, I nervously got on the drum set.

Although my knees were shaking, the atmosphere inspired me to play the best I could. Soon my knees stopped shaking and I regained my composure.

I recall that Jesse Jackson was preaching Pentecostal style—I just loved it. He looked back at me with a huge smile—what a relief—as he called for an offering for the union and César. I stayed on drums as Willie Brown came to the podium right after Jesse, and he also called for offerings.

My family, *Flor Del Pueblo*, and I played for a block party put on by the people on my street in Willow Glen. After the set, a neighbor introduced himself to me, and asked me to audition for the Latin Jazz Ensemble at San José State. My response was, "I work during the day and I'm unable to make band rehearsals."

As luck would have it, a few months later I was hired by the California State Labor Commissioner's Office which was located two blocks from the San José State Campus. This allowed me to take up my neighbor's offer to audition for the band and I was selected as a *timbal* player, an instrument with which I had limited experience.

To make rehearsals, my boss at that time—a Latino ex-Marine—gave me a flexible schedule. That assignment was very challenging in that my sight-reading skills were limited, but as a kid and as a young adult I had heard the book of songs the band played for several years—the repertoire was familiar. The next thing I did was to call my teacher and close friend Luis Carranza for *timbal* lessons. As he had several sets of *timbales* at his house that he could use to teach me technique for the band's songs, he agreed to mentor me. Luis was a person with natural talent on drums, Latin percussion, and vocals. He had played with all the major Latin Jazz bands in the Bay Area—while he didn't read music—Luis rested solely on his memory for complex percussion patterns.

The following week, we practiced to tunes played on his stereo. Then, the stereo speaker began to malfunction, so Luis yelled out to his brother roommate, "Hey, get me a butter knife or something, hey" so he could adjust the speaker connection. That day, he sold me a set of vintage Leedey solid brass *timbales* that he had picked up from Vince Guaraldi's band drummer for $90 dollars. And, giving me the provenance for the equipment, he explained that "the heads were torn by a local player, Gibby Ross, brother of Santana's *timbal* player Karl Perazzo."

As I mentioned, Luis played with the best from the San Francisco Mission District and would be often called to accompany big name performers like Chucho Valdez and Orestes Vilato. Luis was a great support, given the times he turned down gigs with big-name salsa bands over his commitment to local talent. To this day, he continues to be a dear friend, teacher, and musical influence. I still call on him for information about certain traditional Afro Cuban rhythms. In response, he sings the part out and I copy them down in a transcript. In my view, he is a community repository of Afro Cuban musical knowledge.

To play with the San José State (SJS) Latin Jazz Ensemble, and prior to public performances, I practiced its repertoire of songs hour-upon-hour. The payoff came when the band was asked to accompany the San José Symphony in a community performance. Other venues in which we played included the Santa Cruz Kuumbwa Jazz Club, a few local San José night clubs, and the Monterey Jazz Festival.

On the second semester of my time with the ensemble, I went to check out new musicians who were auditioning for the band. I asked the Director how it was going, and he said, "we have an excellent conga player auditioning." This was disappointing for me as I had my eyes on that position. Still, I waited out in the hallway talking to the band's lead singer who mentioned he knew the conga player. They played in high school together and had studied at a music school in Indiana. When the audition ended, the conga player came to speak with the singer.

When I saw him, he looked familiar, I just felt like I knew him and asked his name, followed by "What are your parents' names?" It turned out that he was Willie—my first cousin's son. I had not seen Willie since he was three years old, and now he was twenty-five.

The following semester I was on the *timbal*, and he was on conga. He was an excellent musician, played multiple instruments and sang very well. He gave me sight reading lessons to lessen my struggle with reading the charts when we rehearsed. Eventually, I invited my long-lost relative to dinner at my home and let my wife and kids know who he was and how we were related. He was also a trained chef and cooked up some magic in our humble kitchen.

As we developed a closer relationship, one thing kept tugging at me, so I finally asked him "Can I give your phone number to your mother?" He took a quiet moment and agreed. They had been separated almost all his life, and I knew this was a big decision for them. A few weeks later, my long-lost cousin went to visit his mother in the Seattle area. She called to thank me for the re-connection and said that she always knew, "God would bring my son back." The three of us have been very close ever since. All I can say was "Look at God!"

After a lifetime of musical performances in the San José area, my family and I moved to Ohio. There, my daughters went to a private bible college.

Once we were settled in Ohio, I auditioned as percussionist at the school's church—a Black Pentecostal mega-church—and I began my gospel music journey. I played with the band once on Wednesday and twice on Sunday, as well as at several camp meetings that featured major gospel artists where I had the good fortune to play for many artists and preachers. In addition, I played at Capital University's music conservatory as a Latin percussionist.

On one of several dates, I played with Ndugu Chancler, who, at a very young age, played with Miles Davis, Willie Bobo, and in the 1980's was Santana's drummer. Chancler, a professor at the University of Southern California (USC), taught movie soundtrack production and is famous for recording the drum introduction to "Billie Jean" by Michael Jackson and worked on the soundtrack for "The Color Purple."

In between classes, Chancler and I chatted. I found out he attended the same Community College as my cousin, and he lived in the same neighborhood of Compton, as my Army Medic in 'Nam, Nathaniel "Dumpy" Jones.

While in Ohio, I also played at another large Evangelical church as a Latin percussionist. It was there that I was able to break into the local *salsa* scene. I was linked to *Latino* band leaders by a great friend and Puerto Rican percussionist with whom I did a few gigs and asked, "Where in Puerto Rico are you from?"

Every time he asked, I would reply, "I am Chicano from California."

His retort was "You play and sound like a Puerto Rican."

I took that as a compliment, even though I knew Chicanos had knowledge and always played Puerto Rican music.

Metaphors of life emerge as I walk this daily life. We earned the nicknames we receive and give others along the path.

MY NVA PRISONER AND GROUND SQUIRRELS

Some time ago I turned seventy-four. To celebrate, I asked for a fun and intimate meal with my family at home—Chicago fire thin crust pizza, pumpkin pie from Costco with whipped cream, and Italian roast espresso. I thought about it the day before during my 2-3-mile daily trail walk in my area. I chose to walk over running because it's less painful and more enjoyable.

I recently heard from Ed Cook, a former ARP Squad leader who confirmed that our platoon call sign was Raider, that the Platoon Commander Lt. Douglas P. Rich was Raider 6, and that I was the Squad Leader for First squad, making me Raider One. To the best of my recollection, the most common assignment for the ARP's were Base Camp Raids—that's exactly what they were. To carry those out, we would be inserted by helicopter to suspected North Vietnamese Army (NVA) base camps found all along the Cambodian border or just across the border. Our task was to confirm the location of the base camps, enter, and clear enemy emplacements with grenades. Then we were to search for booby traps, documents, weapons, food, equipment, and people in the camp.

On an early morning base camp raid, I was given the ARP's nickname of "Goober." I was walking point into the camp with another ARP behind me called Gomer. We had cleared all the bunkers in the camp and were leaving the area. When we were finished, I looked down and to my right close to the edge of a bunker when an NVA soldier popped his head out of a very small hole in the ground alongside a large bunker. I pointed my rifle a foot or so from his head. He responded to my directions. He came out and

Getting Ready for a Raid

Garcia and POW

stood up slowly and raised his hands—I have a photograph that one of my guys took of the prisoner and myself.

As expected, I radioed headquarters clearing to take my prisoner for a ride—for an intelligence interrogation. We made our way to an extraction point then flew into the rear area at Quon Loi Base Camp. My guys took photos of him smoking a cigarette, standing in the middle of my squad—I also have a photo of that. Later that day, the ARP's celebrated a little and one of them called out, "Hey Goober, good job!" The guys all cracked up because Gomer and I had been the first guys to enter the base camp. Since then, with fellow ARPs and their families, that name has stuck with me.

One of the memories I'll never forget are those tunnels that moved NVA soldiers to various locations without being detected. Several times while hiking I have been reminded of that NVA soldier whenever a ground squirrel pops it's head out the nest—like squirrels these soldiers were burrowed in tunnels with holes in the ground to surface from their hiding place. The squirrels in my area are dusty brown in color and have big eyes that stare right at you. Most ground squirrels along the trail will freeze and then make furtive motions before running away. But not this little brown buggy eyed NVA squirrel. I could have killed the NVA, and I would've received praise by my guys. But I didn't.

During my walks, I avoid unpaved trail edges because these make crunching sounds as I step down, and the sound triggers sharp reenactments of hand-to-hand combat in 'Nam. In therapy, although I've been told that the best thing to do with PTSD is to face the source of anxiety—I can't always do it. Most often than not, I go further into the vortex created by the episode, and the sickness begins all over again.

The experience I have described with PTSD episodes, which I refer to as a vortex, is like a series of songs, stories, plays or poems that create themes intended to be performed in sequence.

In my case, it was combat.

War was the flower and song that emerged in battle—*fue mi Flor y Canto creado en la batalla*. From this perspective, it is the

Flor y Canto I learned while performing with Chicano groups in California inside the pre-Columbian concept called "*In Xochitl, in Cuicatl*"—a Nahuatl saying that captures the creative in the metaphor for flower and song. Many believe this view of life reflect poetry, but it is also inspiration, breath, and justice. Attributed to Aztec nobility flower and song refers to sacred hymns, chants, and sounds inspired by animistic beliefs for communing with nature. It is a sense of creative magic that one can make something from nothing—a departure from narrow human centric viewpoints.

This awareness of life conditions of all that is perceived and exists in the invisible world suggests that the creation story is now and has always been in a state of flux. These roots are in me, in my Indigenous DNA, that are often at war with modern Euro-centric psychotherapy.

There are more ways to know and understand us and the world. *Flor y canto* is but one of many.

AQUÍ ESTOY—STILL SURVIVING

During my military service noteworthy spiritual changes most vividly began during the U.S.'s Cambodian Invasion period in 1970, when we went in and out of Cambodia and Vietnam. This began after a daytime L-shaped ambush along a "speed trail," or one raised body of earth beaten down hard to allow quick foot travel. The L-shaped ambush was activated by my sniper, whose last name was Mackey. I heard him set off two claymore mines or anti-personnel mines as he fired several rifle rounds into the "kill zone." This was an area entirely covered by direct and effective fire, an element of an ambush with which an approaching enemy force was trapped and destroyed.

Several of these blitzes were deployed by our troops.

This mission resulted in at least three NVA soldiers being seriously wounded. One left a blood trail leading westbound away from the ambush kill zone. Two others were laying on the trail near death. In emplacements along the trail, we quickly avoided being overrun by NVA. It was the area where we more than likely heard all the sounds of the ambush activity. Still, I hurriedly followed my platoon commander's instructions to "do what I had to do and dump the bodies."

Those nights when I can't sleep, I find myself as if I am placing my knees on one of the NVA's elbows, sitting on his chest. Then, he began to fight me. So, I mimic the movement of stabbing him in the throat, watch him twitch and die. This was so traumatic I buried what I had done until Mackey's questioned and reminded me of it.

"Do you know what you did?"

My Squad on Break

The question brough the episode to mind, recalling that I rolled the now dead soldier into a hole along the trail, and I got on my feet, and prepared to leave the area. My platoon leader then directed me to take the group to a nearby stream which we were to follow East bound to our helicopter extraction point about four kilometers east of the ambush site.

While in the river, I noticed a rather large water snake swimming alongside me in the same direction as it raised its head to the surface, turning its eyes right at me, then toward the front and then slither off. This encounter raised my interest in what I recognized as having to do with my Indigenous spirit.

Soon after the ambush and river experiences, I began to see myself, the NVA soldier and the water snake in vivid daytime delusions and nighttime dreams. There seemed to have been some type of non-verbal communication between the three of us.

Gloria E. Anzaldúa, in *Borderlands La Frontera* (2015) argues that there exists an embodied subconscious practice to reincorporate the spiritual back into the body, claiming that the body retains latent, intuitive, 'spiritual' knowledge reawakening abilities that we have and have lost due to conquest and colonization. These dormant knowledges and abilities are reactivated and reawakened during moments of shock and upheaval, which send consciousness traveling beyond the material bounds of the body and brought back into present time and space.

In some of the ambush dreams I continue to experience, I see myself shedding my skin like the water snake does. In those flashbacks, it is but a brief period of reliving that memory, and it borders on the physical and the spirit world. Auditorily the dream/nightmare contains a low moan from the NVA soldier as he said goodbye, while he departed the physical world. The snake is a protagonist in several dreams and stares at me then guides me downriver as if to take me to where I was to be extracted by helicopter.

I experienced an embodied sort of time-travel to the different time and space of that memory—these events are not imagined because what is experienced in the body is real. Such "bodily and boundary violations" bring us into new ways of seeing and being, and "shock us into new ways of reading the world" (Anzaldúa 2015, 86).

A working definition of Indigenous spirit provided by Wong et al. (2006, drawn from earlier work by Benson et al), suggests that "the intrinsic human capacity for self-transcendence, in which the self is embedded in something greater than the self, including the sacred," which motivates "the search for connectedness, meaning, purpose, and contribution." In this context, spirituality is contrasted with religiosity and defined as "one's relationship with a particular faith tradition or doctrine about a divine other or supernatural power" (Benson et al., 2003).

My warrior spirit is not a dream but a reminder of who I am, specifically as it pertains to my Chicano identity. I am a Chicano Native who has constantly remained the same since childhood. Family never lets me forget my Yaqui heritage. They do it in such a way that I would never doubt them.

José Luis Serrano Nájera argues that Indigenous social movements in the Americas have multiple sources. However, regarding Mexican Americans, Chicana/o assertions of cultural Indigeneity, this intrinsically parallels and relates to Chicana/o participation in transnational struggles. This includes communities that recognize Chicana/o participation in broader Native Peoples' movements in the Americas to uphold their rights to self-determination.

In that respect, *Flor del Pueblo*, whose repertoire was exclusively *"Música de las Americas,"* was active in the mid-70's American Indian Movement (AIM) in fundraising musical performances on invitation from founder Dennis Banks in support of the 1973—armed occupation of Wounded Knee, and in opposition to federal policies and practices. Some members of *Flor del Pueblo* were later invited by Dennis Banks—Ojibwe, and Turtle Clan member—to participate in traditional Sioux ceremonies on native land. AIM lead the occupation of Alcatraz Island in 1969, where numerous Chicano activists participated. This supports Nájera's point that Chicana/o activist contributions to anti-colonial and decolonial movements like AIM demonstrate implications of historic Indigeneity.

My lived experiences in East San José has allowed me to witness Chicano active assertions of our right to self-determine and to embrace my native heritage, inspiring me to further investigate the historical implications of cultural continuity in Mexican and Chicana/o communities. As such I learned to become a member of a transnational Pan-Indigenous communities in the Americas through cultural ceremony. I have been fortunate to be a Chicano musician and community activist in such ceremonies.

LAS GUADALUPANAS OF MENUDO HALL

I was raised in a Native and Chicano Catholic household. My church in East San José, California was Our Lady of Guadalupe (OLG). At about the age of six, my first pastor was Father Donald McDonnell who was also César Chávez's mentor. Together they fought and advocated for the rights of the poorest in an area of San José now recognized as the heart of Silicon Valley.

The ethnic make-up of my church included the brown skinned, poorest of the poor, Mexican and Native residents of the neighborhood. OLG was located on Kammerer Street and Sunset Avenue in the Mayfair District of San José, previously called *Sal Si Puedes* or Get Out If You Can. Our community lacked paved streets, sidewalks, and a sanitary sewage waste system, and was populated and maintained by the broad-shouldered working class. Through César's and Father McDonnell's community organizing, the area put pressure on local governments for much needed services and they got them.

In our church, my mom was an active member of a service organization known as *Las Guadalupanas*. It was mostly Mexican American women who provided leadership and addressed social concerns, along with performing necessary works of charity. My mother wasn't the only one involved, both my parents were totally immersed in the *Guadalupanas'* special ministry known as the *Menudo* Hall.

To carry out this endeavor many calls were made to solicit ingredients for making *menudo colorado* or red *chile menudo* to sell after each Sunday Mass. Often, I heard the adults carrying

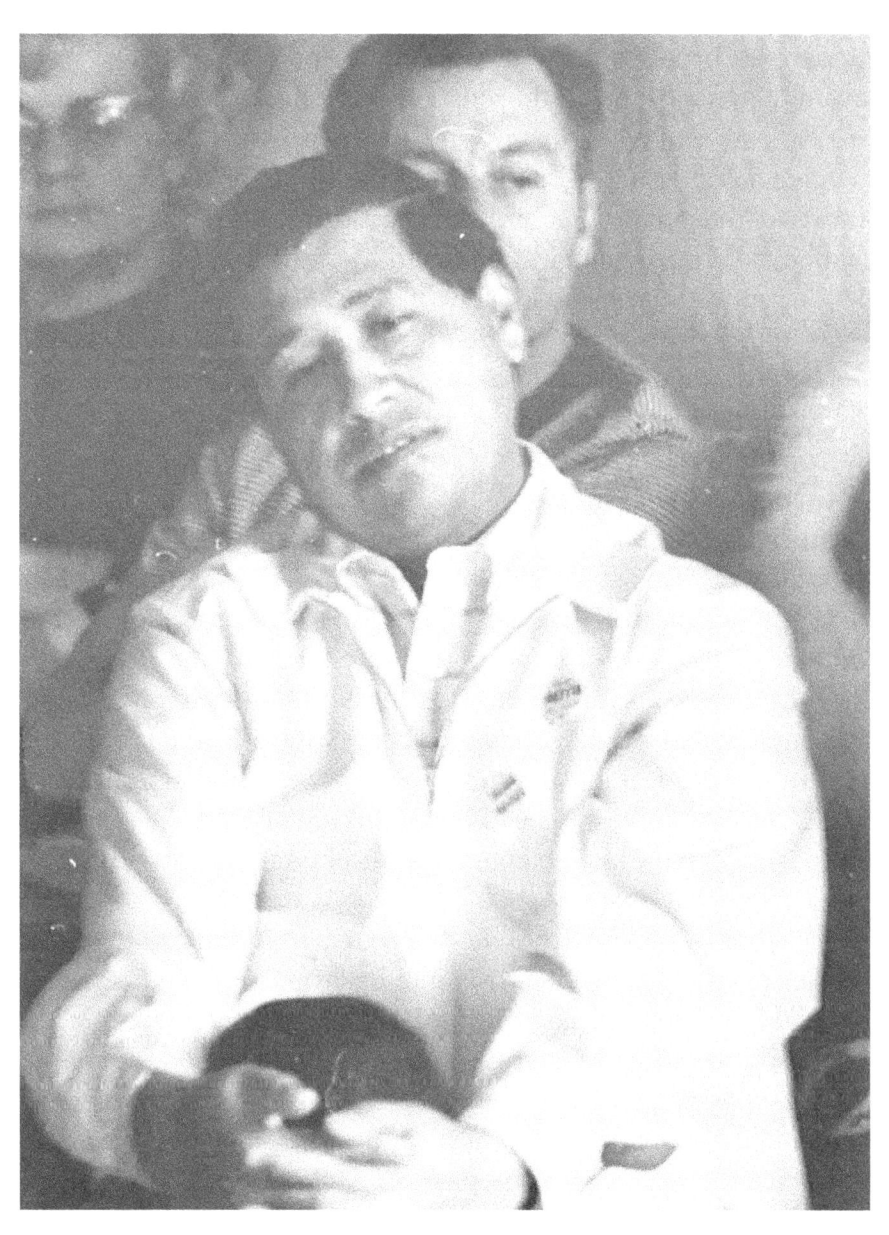

César Chávez at Eastside Community Meeting

out their campaigns on the telephone, asking local merchants for the required ingredients. When they gathered what they needed, my parents brought these ingredients to our house where they carefully washed and prepared the beef p*anza*, broth, hominy, lime, onions, cilantro, oregano, and *chile* peppers.

Menudo takes a long time to prepare, since the meat consists of three of the four stomachs of beef cattle—after it was cleaned, it was cooked in boiling hot water in a large pot with spices and ingredients that would remove its strong odor and tenderize it. When it was done, the *menudo* was taken out of the pot and allowed to cool before cutting or dicing it into smaller strips. Then, the water was discarded, and the meat was returned to the pot with fresh water, adding oregano, red *chile* powder, lime or lemon, hominy, to continue cooking at medium heat. For authenticity, one item my dad insisted on adding was *las patas* or beef hooves. The hominy was last, and its aroma was quite a relief from the smell of *panza*.

In the morning, after passing my dad's taste test, mom and dad loaded a couple of large pots into our white and green '56 Chevy station wagon and took it to the church—a few blocks away. This ministry raised thousands of dollars for OLG, and the funds were used to cover both church benevolence and operational costs. That was one way our Brown Church served the marginalized Native and Chicano communities of East San José. But we would also engage in prayer.

My siblings recently told me that our parents urged them to pray for my safe return from 'Nam. I believe it was their prayers that allowed me to overcome my battles, real or imagined.

Later, I would learn that my Brown Church was one of many led by social justice pioneers. It is a prophetic ecclesiastical community that has contested racial and social injustice in Latin America and the USA for the past 500 years. In every instance of racial and social injustice in Latin America and the U.S., my Brown Church rose to challenge the religious, socioeconomic, and political status quo, including the Spanish Conquest and Spanish colonialism, caste system, Manifest Destiny and US settler colonialism in the Southwest, Latin American dictatorships, and US imperialism in Latin America, as well the oppression of farmworkers, and the exploitation of the marginalized and undocumented immigrants.

I believe my Brown Church has done all this work in the name of Jesus, supporting a theology that embraces a social identity for Latino Christians who are conscious and passionate about social justice. Our brownness reflects the racial liminality of being in between two or more worlds, along with the meaning of being located in the periphery of society. Mexican descent people have lived and continue to reside in the United States since the Mexican American War of 1848— being wanted and unwanted at the same time. To date, these hateful narrative fuels the white nationalist violence that fomented the worst modern mass slaughter of Latinos, August 3, 2019, at the Walmart in El Paso.

As I continue to deal with my life experiences, I am thankful for the lessons. From the good came better times, and in the bad there are lessons that continue to teach me to embrace life in my aim to do the best I can. Guided by the legacy of our ancestors, with the women in my life, Debbie, and my dearly beloved daughters— Frida and Elia and my grandchildren, I continue to pave the way for a better and brighter future.

War did not kill my spirit. It distorted my notions of reality.

Without the support and the love that I have from family, friends, and community, as well as the musicians that continue to inspire me to share my talent, I would be lost living the life of a lesser human being, crashing, and imbibing in substances that intoxicate and numb my mind to what I have experienced as a working-class Chicano who shares an agricultural past with my ancestors. Whatever direction I take in life, I recognize that I must deal with the trauma and spiritual, physical, and emotional pains of war.

Mi Familia

TRUTH AND LIES OF WAR

Although sixty years have passed, there is still much misinformation about combat in Vietnam. Where I fought for the rights of enlisted personnel or grunts to expose the power held by high-ranking officers in command, and I still did my best to do my duty as a soldier and human being.

Like millions of Viet 'Nam combat veterans diagnosed with PTSD, one memory of the events occurring on December 29, 1968, remain inscribe in my conscience. It just won't go away.

I do recall being told by command elements and AFVN Radio, that that there was a cease fire in effect at the time, even though active warfare was taking place. I had been promoted to Sergeant two weeks prior while assigned as an Infantry Squad Leader with the First Platoon of A Co. 2nd Bn. (Mech) 2nd Inf Regiment of the US First Infantry Division. Our assignment had been to provide security for an engineer unit conducting land clearing with heavy tractors called Rome Plows.

On that morning, at about 9:00 a.m., we were dispatched to a nearby streambed to assist a Light Observation Helicopter taking enemy fire from an emplacement at the streambed. At the streambed, my squad which included a Lieutenant, his radio operator, myself, my medic and one other squad member, were tasked with dismounting our APC and assaulting the enemy emplacements. A few minutes after starting the assault, the radio operator was shot and killed just as he was handing the radio handset to the Lieutenant. It became impossible to retrieve the radioman's body until some hours later.

It was not a practice that my squad alone were the only troops in the streambed taking any action amidst RPGs, machine guns, and automatic weapons. After a regroup and second assault, I shot one enemy soldier in the emplacement. This kill was confirmed to me later that day by a fellow squad member.

During a lull in the fighting, I had to drag two wounded NVAs out of the same stream. Although their weight made it nearly impossible, I pulled them from their legs to get them to the stream bed to be processed as POW's and receive medical treatment. While the dragging resulted in banging their heads on rocks in the stream, I felt no remorse—they were enemy combatants. Yet, I wished for their drowning death, placing me in a conflicted state of mind, particularly because I had been shooting at the NVA soldiers who had been firing AK 47's, RPG's, and machine guns at my squad. Also, they had killed my radio man, while we waded toward their emplacement. Given what I have experience in war, the narratives exist between truth and lies that surface in battle.

The media has given much misinformation about combat in Vietnam. This was true in this action. Still, I fought for the rights of enlisted personnel or grunts to expose the power held by high-ranking officers in command, and I did my best to do my duty as a soldier and human being.

With my eyes and mind wide open, I've have gauged the motivation of those who chose to be untruthful in their accounts. These contradictions inspired me to tell my story, particularly when pulling troops and wounded enemy out of that stream where our radio operator was killed. Decades later, we would learn that those who served at the same time, with more authority than us, would claim a protagonist role in the event to cite that victory for their war record, fabricating their involvement in the firefight for self-gain undermining my squads' actions.

After conducting in-depth research, I have come to the realization that these so-called war heroes appropriated the truth about what my squad and I had done. Their interest in obtaining promotions and receiving medals and awards distorted our contributions to embellish theirs. It was their aim to influence the decision makers or those who recommended awards in their favor. For example, there was one leader who presented himself as the hero that came to rescue my squad, arguing that nothing had taken place until he and his unit arrived, without recognizing that we had originally been dispatched to clear the area, rendering us invisible and insignificant, while claiming that those who initially responded were helpers at best.

Given the evidence I've uncovered, it's clear that this individual's primary motive for misrepresenting the incident was purely for self-gain. The men of 1st squad were doing their duty, doing their part for the country—yet their contributions had been distorted and erased in the creation of a sham.

For instance, after futile attempts to recover the body of my radio operator from the stream, I remember having to drag two wounded NVA out, to arrest them as prisoners. Yet, I wished for their drowning death, placing me in a conflicted state of mind, particularly because I had been shooting at the NVA soldiers who had been firing AK 47's, RPG's, and machine guns at my squad, especially because they had killed my radio man, while we waded toward their emplacement.

When we reached the stream bed, one prisoner tried to speak and sit up. Another sergeant and I pointed our weapons at him and yelled for him to stay down. Shooting the prisoner certainly crossed my mind but I concluded this was not the humane thing to do. The loss of one of our men in combat had drained my body and soul many times, but I chose to do the right thing. After all was done, a drink of pre-sweetened Kool Aid from my canteen calmed me for the immediate moment. Still, I live inside the horror of those memories when I recall finding my man's body right close to where he slipped out of my Lieutenant's hands, hanging on some brush about two feet under the water, while the troops expressed the satisfaction of having "done a job on him."

Decades later, we would learn that those who served at the same time, with more authority than us, would claim a protagonist role in the event to cite that victory for their war record, fabricating their involvement in the firefight for self-gain as they undermined our actions.

After conducting in-depth research, I have come to the realization that these so-called war heroes appropriated the truth about what my squad and I had done. Their interest in promotion and receiving medals and awards distorted our contributions to embellish theirs. It was their aim to influence the decision-makers or those who recommended awards in their favor. For example, there was one leader who presented himself as the hero that came to rescue my troop, arguing that nothing had taken place until he and his unit arrived, without acknowledging that we had originally been dispatched to clear the area, which made us invisible and insignificant, as he claimed that those who initially responded were helpers at best—yet their interest was to create sham heroes. What we have experienced evidence that incidents such as this rob warriors of ethnic and class differences from receiving the recognition for their valor in war. Our stories must be told.

REAL AND FABRICATED ACTIONS OF WAR

Narratives of war are complicated. Most often these stories are told to support a privileged perspective or to advance someone's career. However, the stories of foot soldiers like me seldom appear in print.

Throughout the years, in conversations with my guys, some have recalled or given me alternative narratives, as they remember the difficulty of rescuing or recovering the bodies of those that were wounded or lost in Viet 'Nam. One remembered the difficulty of recovering a body because of their inability to maneuver the water. Another recalled me rendering aid to a wounded soldier that was shot in the right forearm, and still other remembered the retrieval of two wounded enemy soldiers. To my credit, they pointed out that I did it without help, as the situation froze them in place. And the rescue was interrupted by the 11th CAV Helicopter that landed near their location. Another member recalled that I redirected my "squad to re-enter the stream, conduct a fire round, and maneuver assault on the enemy positioned in a bunker on the opposite bank," pointing out that "he took aim at an enemy soldier who was about to fire on the first squad, shooting the enemy in the head ... as helicopter gunships began rocketing runs on the enemy bunker."

Among the books written about Vietnam, questions have been raised as to whether the above actions took place.

Yet, countless untold stories impart perspectives and experiences of boots on the ground. Unspoken testimonies from those who since departed kept their secrets of war silent. Clear and truthful narratives may yield lessons that could keep the United States from going to war.

PARTIAL STORIES AND INVISIBILITY OF ETHNIC TROOPS

In this book, I argue that some recollections about Viet 'Nam are distorted and flawed.

Some narratives were written in retaliation for refusing those with more authority to take control of the troops in reaction to ambushes. An alternative "truth" must allow other stories to come to light.

According to John J. Mearsheimer's (Dame, http://sites.ne.edu) in "Truth and Politics" *lying* occurs when a person makes a statement that he knows or suspects to be false in the hope that others will think it is true. Moreover, a lie is a positive action designed to deceive the target audience, as lying can involve making up facts that one knows to be false or denying facts that one knows to be true. But lying is not only about the truthfulness of particular facts. It can also involve the disingenuous arrangement of facts to tell a fictitious story. Specifically, a person is lying when he uses facts—even true facts—to imply that something is true, when he knows it's not.

It's impossible to get inside the minds of those who misinterpret the truth or to identify their reasons for writing falsehoods. Clearly, war distorts truths and lives, allowing some to gain from the actions of war, as others lose their humanity and their lives in the process. Such narratives make the boots in the ground invisible, dismissing their contributions to the nation.

THE INTERNAL BATTLE—
ST. MICHAEL AND ME

Then war broke out in heaven; Michael and his angels battled against the dragon. The dragon and its angels fought back, but they did not prevail and there was no longer any place for them in heaven.
—Revelation 12: 7–8

The first time I heard about war was as a first grader at San José Unified School District's Ann Darling Elementary School on 33rd Street and McKee Road. It was then that I began religious education with fellow Catholic classmates. Toward that end, we met Wednesday afternoons at Five Wounds Church located at 1375 East Santa Clara Street. Five Wounds was the Portuguese National Church and stands at the center of Little Portugal—an area that consists of Portuguese residences and business. Services were in English and Portuguese. There, a nun taught us about the Catholic Faith and prepared us for First Communion and Confirmation. We would spend time in the church seated on hard wooden pews. They also sold us a catechism book to memorize prayers and learn about the seven sacraments of the Catholic faith.

Saturday mornings the nuns sternly gave us direction in catechism classes. They used a wooden clacker that looked like a large clothes pin, to signal us to be quiet, sit, stand, kneel, and exit the pews. For kids who'd squirm, hit each other, and chew the candy they snuck in, long periods of kneeling were challenging, although images of control were placed all around.

In the entrance was a large marble statue of Christopher Columbus. Seated in the first row of pews on the eastside of the center aisle, which gave me a direct view of another huge marble statue of a muscularly defined St. Michael the Archangel. He had a sword in one hand as he stepped on the head of a serpent-like creature. He was a Catholic superhero fit for Marvel Comics. God knows we needed someone to protect us from the mean superior nun who didn't mind smacking a kid on the back of his head with her wooden clacker, not to mention the atmosphere affected by Christopher Columbus. We were praising God in the presence of an idol, of the master colonizer of the Americas, and an original slave trader of Africans and Indigenous Americans in a white church.

From Revelation 12:7–8, the sisters taught us about St. Michael. They explained that a war had broken out in heaven and that Michael, and his angels were dispatched from heaven by God to battle Satan. He and his angels fought back, but they didn't prevail, and Satan and his angels were expelled from heaven. That's how I learned that Michael was a divine badass from way back in the day. He is a spiritual warrior, who stands ready to fight on behalf of good. In retrospect, it was not clear if Jesus walked the same floor as I did in that church. It was a stark atmosphere in contrast to that of my Guadalupe Church. There was no Columbus there, just *Juan Diego* and *La Virgin de Guadalupe*.

A strong believer of the faith, I was one of those guys who always wore some type of Catholic medal in 'Nam. Blessed by the priest and given to me by mom, either St. Christopher or St. Michael hung from my neck. I'm sure other soldiers wore them, but these were the ones given to me. St. Christopher the saint of the traveler protected me, but to me St. Michael seemed more relevant in 'Nam.

His prayer calls for St. Michael the Archangel to defend me in battle; be my protection against the wickedness and snares of the devil. May God rebuke him, I humbly pray, and do thou, O Prince of the Heavenly Hosts, by the power of God, cast into hell Satan and all the evil spirits who roam about the world seeking the ruin of souls. War was hell!

The NVA and VC were fighters who could easily ruin your day with ambushes, land mines, incoming mortars and rockets, and helicopter shoot downs. Later, the residuals of combat could ruin our soul.

On patrol or during one of the hundred or so helicopter aerial combat assaults I experienced, I would put my medal in my mouth. The metallic taste of combining saliva and the flavor of metal calmed me down prior to a mission.

The traditional prototype of the *spiritual warrior*, St. Michael's conflicts against evil may at times be viewed as an interior battle. Much like mine at Five Wounds as a kid and later as a combat veteran. Much like the paratroopers, Saint Michael descended from Heaven along with his army of Angels, ready to fight. The army stayed with that imagery and applied it to the airborne forces, thus I considered St. Michael the Patron Saint and the protector of the paratroopers.

History records that the French '1st Parachute Chasseur Regiment' (1 RCP) has officially designated St. Michael as its patron saint in 1943. Father Jego, a military chaplain serving in a battalion of the 1st RCP declared "*St. Michael guides us in battle, both internal and external: these are the battles of our human lives.*" Battles that fluctuate as we come to terms with the struggles of our lives—from San José to Viet 'Nam, and back.

Let me offer that war never leaves you once you've been in it. The horrors we witnessed and the guilt we carry, as a result of the killings and the decimations of those who seek another type of life, stays with us 24/7, unaware that we carry it all inside us. The rationalization that pervades to justify a war that was not ours to fight, as well as carrying the load of being responsible for a war that was lost by those of us who fought for 'Nam is an unbearable burden we carry—whether awake or asleep.

The consequences of war stay with us for life. Some end up better off than others. Those who are too weak to cope become addicted to drugs and alcohol, or chain smoke cigarettes to cope with the agony and depression of war.

War is always with you. It never leaves you.

It is a force that controls those who served and our loved ones to bear emotional, psychological, and spiritual torment to the end whenever that comes. •

SOURCES

Brockie, Teresa N., Morgan Heinzelmann, and Jessica Gill. "A Framework to Examine the Role of Epigenetics in Health Disparities among Native Americans." *Nursing Research and Practice* 2013 (2013): 1–9. https://doi.org/10.1155/2013/410395.

Chávez, Ernesto. "Chicano/A History." *Pacific Historical Review* 82, no. 4 (November 2012): 505–19. https://doi.org/10.1525/phr.2013.82.4.505.

Doyle-Nelson, Theresa. "St. Michael the Archangel - 'Standing as a Reinforcement and a Bulwark.'" National Catholic Register, September 29, 2021. https://www.ncregister.com/blog/st-michael-bulwark.

Dubroff, Henry. "Foreword." *Limoneira: Celebrating 125 Years of Agribusiness Success*. Santa Barbara, California: Pacific Coast Business Times, 2018. https://www.pacbiztimes.com/wp-content/uploads/2019/03/Limoneira2018-FINAL.pdf

Flintoff, John-Paul. "I Told Them to Be Brave." The Guardian, October 15, 2010. https://www.theguardian.com/lifeandstyle/2010/oct/16/norman-morrison-vietnam-war-protest.

Kwon, Heonik. *Ghosts of war in Vietnam. studies in the social and cultural history of Modern Warfare*. Cambridge University Press, 2008.

Jimenez, Teresa Moreno, and Kathleen M Murphy. "The Mexican American Vietnam War Serviceman: The Missing American." Thesis, California Polytechnic State University, 2015.

Magee, Joe. "Just War." Thomistic Philosophy Page, March 8, 2022. https://aquinasonline.com/just-war/.

Mearsheimer, John J. *Why leaders lie: The truth about lying in international politics*. New York, NY: Oxford University Press, 2013.

Moore, Rick. "Behind the Song: Nat King Cole, 'Nature Boy.'" American Songwriter, October 18, 2021. https://americansongwriter.com/nat-king-cole-nature-boy/.

Olson, Kenneth R., and Lois Wright Morton. "Why Were the Soil Tunnels of Cu Chi and Iron Triangle in Vietnam so Resilient?" *Open Journal of Soil Science* 07, no. 02 (2017): 34–51. https://doi.org/10.4236/ojss.2017.72003.

Serrano Najera, Jose Luis. "Chicana/o Indigenous Affirmation as Transformational Consciousness: Indigeneity and Transnational Human Rights Advocacy since the Chicana/O Movement." eScholarship,

University of California, September 6, 2015. https://escholarship.org/uc/item/42p566p0.

Nguyen, Son. "June 11, 1963: The Internationally Shocking Self-Immolation of Buddhist Monk Thich Quang Duc." The Vietnamese Magazine, June 19, 2021. https://www.thevietnamese.org/2021/06/june-11-1963-the-internationally-shocking-self-immolation-of-buddhist-monk-thich-quang-duc/.

Murphy, Susan. "40 Years after the Vietnam War, Families Still Search for Answers." NPR, April 29, 2015. https://www.npr.org/2015/04/29/402642421/40-years-after-the-vietnam-war-families-still-search-for-answers.

O'Connell, Kit. "How the Science of Epigenetics Proves Inheritance of Trauma." Shadowproof, August 27, 2015. https://shadowproof.com/2015/08/27/native-americans-have-always-known-science-proves-genetic-inheritance-of-trauma/.

Pastrana, Guadalupe. "The Yaqui Tribe: An Indigenous Nation in Resistance." Cultural Survival, December 2, 2021. https://www.culturalsurvival.org/news/yaqui-tribe-indigenous-nation-resistance.

Pember, Mary Annette. Intergenerational trauma: Understanding natives' Inherited Pain, 2016. https://amber-ic.org/wp-content/uploads/2017/01/ICMN-All-About-Generations-Trauma.pdf.

Rose, Hilary A. Epigenetics, or why indigenous peoples can't "Just get over it," December 2018. https://www.ncfr.org/sites/default/files/2018-12/epigeneticsncfr.pdf.

Rotch, Elia Maria. "Flor y Canto: Songs of My Inheritance." Chasing Justice, July 29, 2021. https://chasingjustice.com/flor-y-canto-songs-of-my-inheritance/.

Tobar, Hector. "A Witness Is Still Suspicious about Ruben Salazar's Death." Los Angeles Times, February 22, 2011. https://www.latimes.com/local/la-xpm-2011-feb-22-la-me-tobar-20110222-story.html.

Urbanski, Claire. "Gloria Anzaldúa." Political Theology Network, June 29, 2021. https://politicaltheology.com/gloria-anzaldua/.

Wong, Y. Joel, Lynn Rew, and Kristina D. Slaikeu. "A Systematic Review of Recent Research on Adolescent Religiosity/Spirituality and Mental Health." *Issues in Mental Health Nursing* 27, no. 2 (January 2006): 161–83. https://doi.org/10.1080/01612840500436941.

ABOUT THE AUTHOR

In addition to doing eleven years in the Marine Reserves, after returning from Viet 'Nam, Richard T. García worked as a civil servant for thirty-three years in protecting workers' rights at the local and state levels in California and Ohio. Throughout his life, García has worked on his musical presentations and performed for the community, the UFW, and other social justice venues.

CONOCIMIENTOS PRESS

TESTIMONIOS & NON-FICTION

San José to Viet 'Nam and Back (2024)
Richard T. García

Rooted in Clay: Verónica Castillo y su arte (2023)
Josie Méndez-Negrete

Home, Where Memories Wait to be Remembered (2022)
Teresa Villarreal Rodriguez

*Crossing Borders, Building Bridges:
A Journalist's Heart in Latin America* (2020)
Maria E. Martin

The Art of Mariachi: A Curriculum Guide (2017)
Dr. Rachel Yvonne Cruz

Women, Mujeres, Ixoq: Revolutionary Visions (2017)
Claudia D. Hernández

FICTION

A Street of Too Many Stories (2024)
Denise Chávez

Antonio: A Mexican Boy & His Stories (2023)
Jesse Natal Sánchez

CHILDREN'S BOOKS

Dexter the Ducken (2021)
Alette Lundeberg with Illustrations by ash good

Grandpa Lee's Stories: New Mexico to California (2020)
Helen Najera Reyes with Illustrations by Hector Garza.

Love and Monsters in Sofia's Life / Amor y Monstruos en la Vida de Sofía (2020)
Belinda Hernández Arriaga with Illustrations by Verónica Castillo Salas
Spanish Translation by Josie Méndez-Negrete

CONOCIMIENTOSPRESSLLC.COM